THE
INDEPENDENT
HOMESCHOOL

How to Cheerfully and Peacefully Educate an Independent Learner without Getting Stressed Out, Burned Out, or Constantly Irritated

Dr. Fred Ray Lybrand Jr.

THE INDEPENDENT HOMESCHOOL:

How to Cheerfully and Peacefully Educate an Independent Learner without Getting Stressed Out, Burned Out, or Constantly Irritated

by Fred Ray Lybrand Jr.

Printed in the United States of America

First Edition

ISBN: 978-1-7379958-0-7

Unless otherwise indicated, Bible quotations are taken from The Holy Bible, English Standard Version. Copyright © 2016, by Crossway Bibles, Good News Publishers.

KB

KAUFFMAN
BURGESS
PRESS

CONTENTS

Foreword

I'm a homeschool parent too.

What's next? What's next for your children, your family, your work? What's next will plague us all until we have the ability to handle the unknown… WHAT'S NEXT? That ability comes down to a simple skill; knowing how to teach ourselves whatever we need, to conquer the next thing. It might be more of a mindset than a pure skill; but either way, you can get your homeschoolers ready if you'll follow what is next in this book.

It could be a hard book to read, but that's OK. All you really need to do is read it. I'm sharing with you how to think about homeschooling. I know you want lists and 'how to' instructions. I promise, it doesn't matter much to know what to do; what really matters the most is how you think about things. Once your thinking is clear, the actions start coming to mind very naturally. OK, there is plenty to do too, but the real key is to get your mindset straight. This isn't easy given our culture, experiences, and the ever-devolving media, but you can do it. Read, make notes, reflect, and be transformed!

The original 'working title' was The Independent Homeschool: How to Cheerfully and Peacefully Homeschool without Getting Stressed Out, Burned Out, or Constantly Irritated. I wrote this title first, after talking with homeschool moms. Since the super-majority of homeschools have faithful mothers as the guiding force, it seems to get to the point and still says what I'm aiming for in this book. I'm writing to you, the reader, probably a mom, also many dads, so that you …

1. Will succeed like we did in getting your kids (we had 5) plenty-ready for life (whether or not that includes college).

2. Will NOT burnout in the process and give up your dreams for homeschooling.

3. Will NOT stress-out in the day-to-day reality of home education.

4. Will grow to be cheerful, confident, peaceful, and jazzed about life as a homeschool family.

Now, if I pull that off with words, will you do me (and others) a favor and BLAB about this book a lot? I especially need you to go to Amazon and give it 6 Stars (if you can and say honest-and-amazing words)!

AND

While I am a fan of education, I'm not a fan of failure. A failing homeschool is just as grievous to me as a failing school. Yes, I criticize mass education, but I know there are amazing educators and amazing schools; but not mostly. If schools will embrace my critique and suggestions, I'd be a fan. On balance, I'm not a fan, but they're not (mostly) a fan of homeschooling. Their critiques are welcomed, but with Tom Petty, "No, I won't back down." I'm hoping we can all meet at the tree of learning and find agreement. This book is my attempt to show a better way to educate. However, as it stands today, homeschooling is the better vehicle to grow independent learners. Let's go!

SECTION I

GETTING STARTED

Chapter 1

My Promise

I've been around for a while and I've noticed that there is one thing everyone seems desperate for, and that is HOPE. Why are you homeschooling or considering homeschooling? Isn't it about your waning hope of the mass education options around you? Isn't it about the stirring of possibility to offer your own children what they need for a good future?

What is hope? Hope is different from faith, which is being assured about a future outcome. Hope is about possibilities. Hope looks at a future that is positive, possible (if not likely), and yet is not guaranteed. The not guaranteed part is the challenge. We all want guarantees; though life might be pretty boring if we knew everything would turn out (for sure) just as we planned. Instead, hope gives us motivation and energy, without being arrogant about the future. As it turns out, that is quite enough for human beings to make things happen.

In contrast, we who moved into homeschooling see a measure of hopelessness with public and mass education options. Hopeless is clearly an overstatement, since most of us eventually move toward something different than homeschool in the course of time. Just by observation we can see that most parents shift from homeschooling to something else (COOPs, Private Schools, and Public Schools) by the time high school hits. It's not really that we see it as hopeless, but we do see the failing nature of mass education as a cause for deep concern.

What's so bad about mass education in America? Well, it varies from one area to the next, but basically it's about the environment and the education. The environment is morally unsupportive in our way of thinking. Most of us are cautious about the kinds of kids we like our own to befriend. We all know that 'you'll never be like the people you don't hang around', true?

Drugs, violence, promiscuity, weak academics, all of these are a part of the concern, but we aren't naïve. We do know that some kids wind up in AP classes, and some make friends with moral and academic leaders. We know in any environment we are all going to have to determine who we want to model and what we want to accomplish. Mass education environments, however, turn the odds against us. Mass education, as we all know, is also a social engineering experiment growing an army of insecure social justice warriors who neither understand nor honor free speech and individual responsibility.

Where does it go if your child isn't getting the individualized academic attention she needs? What happens when they are bullied or ostracized? What does it mean for your child's development if they can't pray, talk about their faith, and are in constant danger of not saying things perfectly-and-politically-correct? Learning is about becoming mature and emotionally healthy. Do you think the odds are in your favor where you live? Can you afford what it costs financially or emotionally or practically to get your child to be a successful student in a school in your area?

MY PROMISE: You can pretty easily compete with the best of the best schools if you follow the path I'm going to give you here. It's as simple as UNDERSTAND, then ACT. In fact, the action part is hardly worth mentioning. We are going to turn your view of education on its head so you can succeed. Or, if you have already started to figure this education puzzle out, then welcome home!

We are going to unpack for you how to turn your student into his own teacher for the rest of his life. If he learns this skill, then he'll never be without options in life. Lose a job? Big deal…just decide what you want and learn what you need to learn. It sounds like I'm saying this is easy, but there is a little more to it than that. There is some heavy lifting in the beginning, but once it's in motion hardly anything can stop it! Great athletes make things look easy too, but it didn't start there. A slam dunk is easy for an NBA forward, but once upon a time he had to learn it.

Homeschool can get to be easy for you as well, but you've got to transform your understanding of learning in order to create the little learners you want. The aim of this book is to do that very thing; to transform your thinking so your actions as a homeschool parent are obvious to you and impervious to criticism.

Now, what about hope? If you are willing to learn and willing to re-think a few things you are sure about, then everything will change as you consider the knowledge we are handing you here. You can absolutely get your own children ready for life, but you are going to have to become the kind of homeschool parent independent learners need. You might need to get over some of your own stuff, learn a few things about setting up systems, and convince yourself that 'teaching' is NOT what your students need, but 'causing them to learn' is the secret spice in the recipe we offer for home-education.

"The illiterate of the 21st century will not be those who cannot read and write, but those who cannot learn, unlearn, and relearn." — Alvin Toffler

Toffler is saying something important, though a little overstated. It should be that the illiterate will NOT ONLY be those who cannot read and write, but also those who can't learn, etc. Get excited, get ready, get hopeful. It all starts coming together for you today. You can grow independent learners by modeling and giving them the skills they really need to make it successfully in these challenging times.

Chapter 2

Introduction: Systems, Ockham's Lever, & Why You Should Listen to Me

My obsession is your freedom. -Fred Ray Lybrand

Basically, I'm lazy. In fact, you should be lazy too, but you probably don't know how to admit it to yourself and others. I'm not talking about being a sluggard, but I am talking about how ALL OF US really don't want to expend more effort than necessary to get the results we want in the world. In large measure this kind of 'laziness' is why technology can be helpful; it finds the better-faster way.

Allow me to interject a little of my story here to explain my love of lazy. I grew up in a highly competitive home with a mother who was honored as one of the Outstanding Young Women in America while my dad was serving as an Alabama State Senator. Dad was a trial attorney too, and mom was the ultimate plan-your-work-work-your-plan achiever. My older brother and younger sister were both successful in their endeavors (cheerleading, scouting, youth politics, writing, etc.). In this environment, 'succeeding' is not an option. Everything reflects on the family and can cost you votes! The problem, however, was that we had a dark underbelly in our family system; alcohol abuse. If you have ever encountered severe alcoholics, then you should know that the dysfunction of the slavery began long before the problem became apparent. Mom and dad divorced after 27-ish years of marriage, and both of them had major struggles with alcohol. I only mention this to explain the context of my life as a tandem challenge:

1. Be a success

2. Don't let the hidden dysfunction distract you

Frankly, that combination is pretty rough for anyone. There is a huge energy drain when conflict, miscommunication, and aberrant behavior is a part of every day. The challenge is multiplied when the expectations to succeed are idealized despite the noise. If we decided to run for a club vice-president position, mom would ask, "Why not president?" Dad was a bit more about the grades. When I graduated with Honors from my master's program with a 3.62 GPA, Dad asked, "Why didn't you make a 4.0?" It's that sort of thing that drove me to be lazy. I simply couldn't spend the time others could on schoolwork, so I had to learn how to be more efficient, to be quicker in producing results. Laziness is a matter of less energy expended and less action supplied. But what if you are also ambitious? That was my challenge and it set me on a course of discovering the power of lazy! The other gift this family system brought me was that of being independent. In large measure we had to parent ourselves. No word was ever defined without hearing, "Look it up." No paper was ever reviewed or edited or discussed (Dad did like to work with a poem or two). If grades were your problem, then they would make it a critique (though occasionally we did have a tutor added in a crisis).

In homeschooling, Jody and I (and our five students) all worked at finding the lazy (better-faster) way to successfully get everyone educated. After Jody taught them to read, and not counting field trips or 'reading to the kids' time (optional in the later years), we only spent a combined total of 30 minutes a day schooling all five of our children. As they left home one-by-one for college, the time investment got even shorter. By the way, because of how I arranged my life, I too was significantly involved in our homeschooling efforts.

My Obsession (in life): I want a perfect system with a perfect result. The system only has one step. And, that step doesn't involve me!

Yes, I can drive people a little crazy, but that's what I look for and it's why in 21 Lessons, my Writing Course can totally transform the writing of a child who is just a little bit open to learn a radically different way to think about writing. I don't have the energy (lazy) to learn all the grammar, so I discovered and tweaked a way to have good grammar (and punctuation) without knowing the rules. It's linguistics based, but the kids don't need to know linguistics to use it and improve. The Writing Course is the output of my obsession. Of course, this applies to our entire Independent Learner Courses, and these insights are an essential part of the path to successful homeschooling I'm sharing with you right now.

The courses I mention are simply an illustration of the power of lazy; some call it efficiency, but a rose by any other name, etc.

Please be patient with the following material. I'm sort of going 'full nerd' here, but I assure you it is both important and won't last forever. There are three aspects to my obsession with finding the lazy-way to accomplish anything:

1. Systems and Structural Thinking

2. Ockham's Razor

3. Archimedes' Lever

SYSTEMS THINKING

A system is basically a set of interconnected and interacting elements. A structure is slightly different, but often operates in a similar way. Practically, I just think of a system as a structure with moving parts. For our purposes I'm not going to make a big distinction, except to say we are looking at the simple fact that a combination of interacting elements is what causes anything to happen. Writing is a combination of what one intends to say, the words chosen, the grammar involved, the layout on a page, etc. A little more sophistication is to add that this 'interaction' produces a consistent or predictable result of some kind or another. Systems thinking, as you might guess, is simply the process of thinking about things from a systemic perspective. In other words, analyzing what's happening (or what you might want to have happen) by looking at the connected elements or process involved allows you to predict and improve the results. I guess it's complicated, but it really doesn't have to be. For example, a symphony is actually a pretty complicated piece of musical performance that can employ up to 120 performers in four groups of related instruments; woodwinds, brass, percussion, and strings (violin, viola, cello and double bass). Whoa. And yet, they are simply the organized result of a composer writing layer-by-layer. One thing, add another, add another, etc., until it's organized. While I'm kind of out of my domain here, it is a relationship between the beat and the melody that pretty much helps organize the whole thing. In fact, with a few bits in place, it sort of 'writes itself' once it's in motion. It's the same with a screenplay, a novel, or a speech. We can't say, however, that the composer or the beat or the cello 'causes' the symphony.

With this in mind, why wouldn't it apply to homeschooling, parenting, or the efficient doing of laundry? It would! Looking at the connectedness of things begins to change it all for you. You can make your system visible (I use pen and paper) so you can understand it, explain it, and then improve it as a family.

OCKHAM'S RAZOR

Ockham's Razor is a principle from philosophy a British friar famously observed (along with plenty of others over time) in the fourteenth century. The Wikipedia article states it nicely: "Suppose there exist two explanations for an occurrence. In this case, the simpler one is usually better. Another way of saying it is that "The more assumptions you have to make, the more unlikely the explanation is true."

(https://simple.wikipedia.org/wiki/Occam's_razor)

In a similar vein to Da Vinci's observation that 'simplicity is the ultimate sophistication', the razor invites us not to dwell upon complicated explanations as the answer when simpler explanations can make sense of things just as well. Almost any subject can be blessed by Ockham's Razor as a way to think; for example, in writing 'omit needless words' adds to the improvement of any paper or book (thanks Strunk & White). The fires in California in 2017, 2020, and 2021 (and beyond?) are a good example. I saw an article that claimed they were caused by poor forest management practices and climate change. Not to enter the debate, but climate change only complicates (adds to) the explanation. Poor forest management practices (along with the common elements of drought and high winds) are enough to explain the fires. In fact, without climate change the winds can get high enough, and the fuel dry enough, to cause fires (and they have done so in California with great regularity for eons). The reality-or-not of man-caused climate change has nothing to do with looking at the cause of the fires in California. Ockham's Razor simply tells us that the more we add assumptions, the more likely we are moving away from what really explains the event or situation.

In thinking this way, it allows us to stay true to the essentials. Homeschooling (and all education) is most fundamentally about READING, WRITING, and ARITHMETIC. I'm guessing you've heard that before, but it is on target. Reading allows us to expand our vocabulary, and to tap into the great minds of history and ideas to acquire knowledge when we need it. Math is the language of science and teaches logic (and absolutes) to students who live in a logic-needy world. Writing forces us to clarify our thoughts with an eye on communicating effectively with others. Communicating with others is how we make use of information and ideas to accomplish great things together.

Do people need more than the Three R's? Kind of...no! Someone skilled in these things can quickly acquire the knowledge or additional abilities needed for a greater endeavor. But, if one or more of these is lacking, then there isn't much of a chance to move forward in the education-dependent areas of life and our world. What makes for an 'educated student'? Ockham's Razor would say that someone skilled in reading, writing, and arithmetic is likely close to the answer. We can add morality training, or something to do with the arts, but the more we add the further away from the answer we get. So much of mass education today is obsessed with tedious trivia that it gets in the way of the profound essentials that lead to the genuinely educated student. The three R's is the foundational skill stack that allows your students to build an even greater skill stack.

ARCHIMEDES'S LEVER

Archimedes was a prolific Greek mathematician, engineer, and astronomer who is identified with what is simply called the Lever. His most famous quote on the insight is,

Give me but one firm spot on which to stand, and I will move the earth.

(The Oxford Dictionary of Quotations)

He is describing the power of leverage, which is the mechanical advantage found in using a lever. This advantage, in a way, multiplies energy so that greater work is done with less effort expended. Commonly, imagine a boulder being moved by a branch, a smaller rock, and a person. He was saying the same thing applies to moving something as large as the earth. A place to stand (and a long enough board with a fulcrum) means little 'ole him could move the whole thing! He used this insight to develop such things as the screw pump, compound pulleys, and defensive war machines.

The practical use of leverage means that we are looking for a relatively smaller thing that creates a multiplied result when it is used. In education, you want to think of something like vocabulary. Vocabulary is easily thought of as a learn-a-word-at-a-time effort. However, when you think of leverage, you can discover that Latin roots (for English) can produce the effect of knowing ten extra words for each root one learns. That is leverage!

"OCKHAM'S LEVER"

Okay, this is my term for what I like to do…my obsession, if you will. Consider the term 'Ockham's Lever' as coined by me (with some help from Scott Walls – kudos) from now on. Ockham's Lever combines the idea of **(1) parsimony** (the fewest elements which satisfy an explanation of how something works) and **(2) leveraged focus** on that which causes a greater effect compared to the effort required. All this means is that I look for the least number of elements necessary for a result, and focus on the most impactful of those elements as a point of concentrated effort. I'm not saying I'm the grand-master of Ockham's Lever, but simply thinking this way creates pronounced changes for the things I touch with it. Here's the simple sequence I use daily:

SEE

SIMPLIFY

SEPARATE

SOLVE

When I look at anything, I want first to SEE what is there. I might see one of our young readers not reading well out loud. I might notice a little more that he is guessing at a word, rather than sounding it out. Next, I want to SIMPLIFY what I'm looking at; which often means that I dismiss psychological explanations for issues with parenting and education. Why do I need to guess at fear or self-image issues when they really aren't necessary to explain things? When I simplify the story it's just a matter of sounding out the parts of a word, hearing it said, then deciding which actual word is being used. Next, I make sure to SEPARATE problems from realities. Problems always suggest that there is a solution, while some realities can't be solved at all. Spending time and energy attempting to solve something that can't be solved is just a fool's errand. So, in this example, the SOLUTION was pretty obvious: Teach each child to sound out words they do not know BEFORE they guess the word. I'm sure this is a part of most phonics programs, but we had to refine it for our learning readers. In fact, they should be sounding out every word as they read until they're no longer guessing.

Consider questions as another example. Questions are amazing and profound points of leverage, and are a simpler explanation for how we humans come up with amazing insights at the speed of thought. Here's a link for an award-winning article I wrote on creating better questions: https://independenthomeschool.com/betterquestion. The basic idea is that if you ask a question which sets in motion a tension-seeks-relief dynamic where the questions we ask look for specific kinds of answers. In the example I use concerning the invention of glass cooking containers, the question was, "Glass breaks… can't you do something about that?" From there researchers invented dozens of ways to keep glass from breaking, and several of them were economically viable. If the question had been, "Why does glass break?" Then all we would have gotten would have been a large report on the physics of why glass breaks! Instead, we now have glass cookware.

When I apply the principle of leverage to the simplicity of questions, I think about an 'ultimate question' that sets everything in motion toward improvement. The question I invented was, "What's the better question?" So, if a question is good and I ask a question to find a better question, then I'm multiplying the effect.

First Question: How do I educate my kids at home?

Better Question: How do my kids get educated at home?

Better Question: How can I get my kids to educate themselves at home?

Better Question: How can I educate my kids to educate themselves for life at home?

Well, you get the idea. Maybe you don't think they are better questions, but the truth is that my sense for improvement says they are 'good enough' for what I'm trying to do. This is why we discovered and improved upon the conviction that education is about helping a student become his own teacher (you'll hear a lot about that in this book).

If the easiest explanation is that students who take on the task of learner are far more efficient when listening to a teacher (or reading a book or working problems, etc.), then it becomes clear that combining the two elements of student and teacher into the one person would be even more efficient. Imagine if the student and teacher were both always available! That's the idea behind Ockham's Lever.

Chapter 3

How to Read this Book

If you skipped to this chapter first, good job! Frankly, I'm giving you permission not to read this book the way you probably feel like you 'should' read it. However, the last chapter is almost among the most important. If you can start making Ockham's Lever (previous chapter) a part of the way you think and approach things, then you're on your way!

Perhaps you've been reading for a long time and have your own approach. If you feel good about how you grasp and use information, then skip ahead. However, if you are open to a few thoughts, then I'd like to share them with you.

Plunder this Book

Years ago, I realized that we all use a cliché when we speak of our reading. The question we ask is, "Have you read [Insert Book Title of Choice Here]?" When we answer "Yes" is where the cliché gets us. Now, a cliché is a popular cultural word or phrase for something that is common knowledge, or ubiquitous (as they say); but that has become underappreciated or misunderstood because of this casual flinging of a phrase. You get what you pay for, the customer is always right, and what goes around comes around are common examples. However, do we really understand and make use of the nature of value, customer care, and cause-and-effect? Do we really get what we pay for, or do we overpay sometimes? Are customers always right? Really, always? Does everyone really 'get what's coming to them' or is there mercy in this world? You see, in general all of these things are true, but we don't really think about the profound things they represent, or the exceptions that 'prove the rule'

Have you read such-and-such book? Yes...ah...No. Read can mean that you looked at every word. Of course, you can also read every word but not understand anything. The real question we should be reaching for is, "Have you plundered such-and-such book?" I coined the idea and phrase of plundering a book some years ago to accurately describe what I'm really trying to do. It also gives me permission to communicate better with friends, colleagues, and clients.

Plundering is borrowed from the picture of swashbuckling pirates of movie fame. They board the victim ship and take all the valuables, leaving the 'junk' behind. Now, isn't that a picture of efficiency. Reading every word doesn't tell the story, but plundering sure does! I like to say, "I worked through the book and got all kinds of valuable insights from it." Or, "I took the stuff I really needed from it, yes, I plundered ('read') it!" Or, finally, "Well, I spent time plundering the book, but I didn't find it helpful, and in some cases I think it was flat-out wrong."

Well, now you have permission to plunder this work. You won't hurt my feelings at all. In fact, I think it's estimated that only 20% of non-fiction books are 'read' all the way through. Non-fiction isn't written or designed to be read all the way through. The dictionary is non-fiction; definitely something we all plunder- but-don't-read!

Go dig in and find the stuff you need. Survey it. Jump around. I promise, your brain can put things in order regardless of what you throw at it. When you get your meal from a cafeteria line, you don't eat it in the order you got it, do you? It's kind of the same. Find what you need. If you want to go through each page and savor it, then do that too. Just don't let it sit on a shelf and rot, or get buried under your 'must read' pile and suffocate.

Use Leverage on this Book

As you know, a lever is something that sort of multiplies work. A plank can move a boulder if it's approached properly. Leverage is that same idea. How do you get more with less? What strategic small changes can have a big effect? In education there are three basic skills that we all know about: reading, writing, and arithmetic. Which of those has the most leverage? Hmm…it's a math and science world, so learning to think with numbers is really important. But, then again, if someone can articulate her thoughts in a clear way with written words, then that really makes one's thinking and impact far superior.

I'm going with reading. Reading is where the leverage is among these three, mostly because you can't do either of the other two without reading. Reading opens a life to the great minds of the world, models how to write, and changes the actual physical structure of the brain to work better. Am I saying the other two are not necessary? Of course not. I am saying that if one doesn't learn to read well, then good luck with math or writing.

Here's where I think the leverage is for this book:

* The Must-Have-Mindset for a Successful Homeschool

* Mental Modeling

These parts are trying to convince you that how you think about homeschooling changes everything. Most of us are looking for actions and applications, but I PROMISE YOU that it's how you think about it that changes everything. If you just read those two parts and then burn this book, you'll still be way ahead of most stressed-out homeschool educators. In fact, just those two chapters could change everything by tomorrow morning if you dare to take them to heart.

That's what I mean by leverage!

Personalize this Book by Taking Notes a Special Way

There are two ways to take notes. You can do it however you want, but you probably are leaking all kinds of opportunities to change for the better. The normal way to take notes is to write down exactly what the speaker or teacher says. Yes, it might be outlined, but the focus is on content. Fine, whatever...how often do any of us go back and make use of these notes? If you are the exception, then bask in it and know that you are pretty much alone on this one. Fortunately, since you have the book, you have the notes.

Here's how I recommend you read this book. Take notes about things that strike you, things you'd like to think about or try on for size. Go to the notes section and write down a summary phrase or quote me. Next to that quote, put the page number or numbers in parentheses. In the course of time you'll have a private collection of the stuff you need. You'll also know where to go to read the whole idea again.

Have you noticed that all books have people who post 'loved it /changed my life' AND people who 'hated it / drivel' / 'everyone knows this' type comments? Why is it that way? I believe the answer is about point-of-need. When you are exposed to an idea that massages a need in your life or answers a burning question, then you'll shout, "Eureka, that's it!" It is at these points, of having a need met that we are most impacted and blessed.

The way I'm suggesting you take notes allows you to not to worry about 'liking' the book, but rather it empowers you to go on a treasure hunt and plunder your burning needs. Taking notes this way encourages you to focus upon, and review, what could really help you the most. Here's an illustration:

The story is told of a Native American who left the reservation for the first time to visit downtown New York City. Walking down a busy street with his friend, he suddenly stopped and said, "I hear a cricket". His friend said, "You're crazy! There's no way you could hear a cricket in all this noise!" He persisted, "No! I hear a cricket... I'm sure of it!"

His friend said, "It's noon! There are thousands of people bustling around, cars honking, taxi cabs squealing around corners, and sirens wailing...I don't believe you can hear a little cricket in all this!" The Native American listened again and walked slowly across the street where he found a large cement planter with a shrub in it. He dug beneath the leaves, and sure enough...there was a cricket!

His friend was stunned, "You've got amazing hearing!" But the man said, "No. My ears are no different from yours. It simply depends on what you're listening to. Here, let me show you."

So, he reached into his pocket and pulled out a handful of change—a few quarters, some dimes, nickels and pennies...and dropped it on the concrete. You guessed it... every head within a block turned! "You see what I mean? It all depends on what you're listening for." -Unknown

I'm inviting you to listen to your own needs and points of stress or challenge. Not to belabor the illustration; I'm providing you crickets and change. There's a reason you need to hear certain things today. The next pass through the book, it'll probably be something different.

SECTION II

MUST-HAVE-MINDSET FOR A SUCCESSFUL INDEPENDENT HOMESCHOOL

Chapter 4

The 5 Must-Have-Mindsets for a Successful Independent Homeschool

Perhaps you already realize that mindset is a big deal with human beings. Mindsets are largely the habitual ways we think, akin to attitude, which influence how we interpret what's happening and how we ultimately respond. Dr. Carol Dweck offers landmark research on the topic concerning what she calls 'fixed' and 'growth' mindsets. Those who develop a fixed mindset tend to react to learning situations with a limited, if not defensive, posture. The perspective of the fixed mindset is one of assuming the one who owns it is essentially smart. While that seems fine on the surface, it has a dire effect in that it implies there is no further learning to do. If IQ, intelligence, or even knowledge is fixed, then new information coming at the individual is either wrong or unnecessary. One of the contributing factors to the fixed mindset is the assurance parents and teachers give children that they 'are smart', rather than praising the effort involved in the learning process.

A growth mindset, as it sounds, is an orientation that growth is desired, important, and possible. A student with this mindset is apt to react to a learning situation with a sober-minded viewpoint that learning anything is possible, though it might take some effort. This mindset is developed by praising effort and progress, rather than by praising a student's identity (smart, dumb, etc.). Instead of producing defensiveness, a growth mindset produces a measure of patience in moving from 'not knowing how' to 'knowing how' the progress we call learning.

The five teaching mindsets we believe are vital, cover two orientations and three distinct aims:

Teaching Mindset 1: The Learning Orientation

Teaching Mindset 2: The Educational Orientation

Teaching Mindset 3: The Parenting Aim

Teaching Mindset 4: The Educational Aim

Teaching Mindset 5: The Management Aim

Teaching Mindset 1: The Learning Orientation

All Learning Involves Two Things: Curiosity & Frustration

I can't tell you exactly where I tripped over this notion, but it seems to deserve the level of a truism. People who learn, the real learners, consistently are insatiably curious. Here's some proof,

John W. Gardner, who died in 2002 at the age of 89, was a legendary public intellectual and civic reformer — a celebrated Stanford professor. His speech on November 10, 1990, was delivered to a meeting of McKinsey & Co., the consulting firm whose advice has shaped the fortunes of the world's richest and most powerful companies. But his focus that day was on neither money nor power. It was on what he called "Personal Renewal," the urgent need for leaders who wish to make a difference and stay effective to commit themselves to continue learning and growing. Gardner was so serious about this learning imperative, so determined that the message would get through, that he wrote the speech out in advance because he wanted "every sentence to hit its target."

What was his message? "We have to face the fact that most men and women out there in the world of work are more stale than they know, more bored than they would care to admit," he said. "Boredom is the secret ailment of large-scale organizations. Someone said to me the other day 'How can I be so bored when I'm so busy?' I said 'Let me count the ways.' Look around you. How many people whom you know well — people even younger than yourselves—are already trapped in fixed attitudes and habits?"

So, what is the opposite of boredom, the personal attribute that allows individuals to keep learning, growing, and changing, to escape their fixed attitudes and habits? "Not anything as narrow as ambition," Gardner told the ambitious McKinsey strategists. "After all, ambition eventually wears out and probably should. But you can keep your zest until the day you die." He then offered a simple maxim to guide the accomplished leaders in the room. "Be interested," he urged them. "Everyone wants to be interesting, but the vitalizing thing is to be interested…As the proverb says, 'It's what you learn after you know it all that counts.'"

In these head-spinning times, even more so than when John Gardner offered his timeless advice, the challenge for leaders is not to out-hustle, out-muscle, or out-maneuver the competition. It is to out-think *the competition in ways big and small, to develop a unique point of view about the future and get there before anyone else does. The best leaders I've gotten to know aren't just the boldest thinkers; they are the most insatiable learners. https://hbr.org/2014/09/the-best-leaders-are-insatiable-learners*

Yes, it isn't ambition or fear that pulls it off, it's an insatiable curiosity. The easiest way to get there is to fall in love with a few questions like those on the top of my own list:

Why?

How does it work?

What if this is true?

Why does this matter?

What could I do with this to make things better?

Why is this important to know?

Is this really true?

Of course, you can create your own set of questions, but they all get down to a way to look at things so as to see them as something that might be useful, that might matter, someday, someway, somehow.

Curiosity alone won't do it, however. When we are involved in learning, we are usually and regularly frustrated. Frustration is understandable since we want something (usually NOW) and can't get it (NOT YET). The irritation that is involved in learning or creating is referred to as *creative tension* by one of my mentors, Robert Fritz. This tension is just interpreted as a bad thing when we are learning. It's the same tension we feel when watching an exciting movie or reading an exciting book. We want to 'know' (learn) what is going to happen, so we stay engaged. This kind of tension, however, is understood in a positive way. Even children who look forward to Christmas morning will say something like, "I can't wait for Christmas to get here!" Well, they can wait, but the distance between NOW and NOT YET is strongly felt.

In learning, it's the same thing. If we are curious, then we want to know. If the subject or skill is a little involved or complex, then it's going to take some time. Helping our students grasp this reality is often crucial in their growth as a leaner. They must grasp that there is absolutely nothing wrong with them because they are frustrated. They must embrace the fact that learning may just simply take some time and hard work!

When our son, Brooks, was shifting from advanced math / pre-calculus to formally taking calculus, I heard him in at the kitchen table expressing some of his frustration with pounding fists and a raised voice. "Calculus is stupid. They don't know how to explain it right," he said (or something like that). I told him that I know it's frustrating, but think about it. "How many problems have you solved in this Saxon curriculum?" I asked. "I don't know," he said. We then got all the textbooks out and counted. Now, since he had corrected all the problems he had missed, the entire number of problems was the number he had solved in his life as a math student. We counted about twenty-nine thousand problems. That number may be off by a thousand, but it's close. In all the years, and through that many problems, Saxon had somehow been right and effective 99.98% of the time! I asked him if he thought calculus was learnable via Saxon Math? He said, "Yes." Brooks then got busy, embraced the frustration, and settled down to learning. In about a year, right at his fifteenth birthday, he completed calculus.

Part of the trick in dealing with the frustration of learning is to simply realize that the solution pre-exists (more on this under **Key 5: Permanent Problem Solving**). In learning, it means that the student reminds himself that this subject can be learned...it has been learned by thousands-upon-thousands of others who are probably less 'smart' than your little learner.

Chapter 5

Teaching Mindset 2: The Educational Orientation

See Education as 98% Skills Acquisition and 2% Vocabulary

This is probably the biggest departure we will make from the current climate in much of mass education. Maybe it comes from trivia games, or television, or social media, but it is obvious that what's in the air these days is that smart people know a lot of stuff. Unfortunately, that isn't really the aim of education. It is a matter of mistaking the effect for the cause. Just knowing a lot of data doesn't mean you can do a lot with it. Instead, we really need to understand the importance of tools the importance of know-how.

Alfred North Whitehead captured the relationship between know-how and knowledge when he said, "Education is the acquisition of the art of the utilization of knowledge." It is the art of utilizing, or using knowledge. Some years ago I had a problem with changing out a spigot in our bathtub. No matter how I worked with it, I could not get a pair of pliers on the nut. I finally gave up and got a plumber. He told Jody, "Your husband could never loosen this without a pipe wrench." Frankly, I had the dual problem of not having a pipe wrench and not knowing what I was doing! Using knowledge is great, but the skills of acquiring knowledge are even more foundational. As mentioned elsewhere, we acquire knowledge through the skills of Reading, Writing, and Math. In effect, these skills organize our minds for learning and using knowledge. Unfortunately, it isn't that we don't know this, rather it is that we don't hold onto the priority of making education fundamentally about growing our knowledge skills. Of course, morality and ethics direct our learning to contribute to society; however, it's the refinement of the vital skills we need that carry us onward to success.

Literacy is an example of where we nobly seem to fall on our own sword. The literacy rate in America matches the world rate at about 86% (Israel, by contrast is 97% or better). However, 'literacy' means what? Depending on where you look, it means the ability to read (and write) at the very least. Unfortunately, that doesn't look at it as a skill on a continuum. Instead, it simply thinks of it in minimal terms. What if the goal of your homeschool was not

~~To have my students be able to read and write (and do math)~~

BUT

To have my students be able to read and write (and do math) WELL

Merely having the mindset to see reading as something one can move toward mastering makes all the difference. Reading is a skill that can improve beyond the minimal. Writing is a skill that can improve beyond OK. Math is a skill that can improve beyond 'pass the test'. I hope you see the wisdom here. Our standard should be 'improve/do even better' rather than just enough to get across the finish line of OK. When you move your mindset to see 98% of what you are trying to do is the development of skills, then everything becomes simpler and focused. You are no longer obsessed with what others think or where your child ranks in a peer group. What you focus on is getting to a better tomorrow than your student experiences today. Today is just a starting place for learning a little more.

A few years ago, I tutored a homeschool student who was moved into a private school and was flunking math (and not doing very well in his other classes either). I went back through his books to find out what he really knew. Basically, he was about three grades behind. Instead of trying to catch him up, I had him go back three grades and start there. Every day he would do a set of problems from three grades back, make corrections, move to the next lesson. We also limited his focus on a reasonable number of problems for about an hour's work. Hard material just meant fewer problems. What did we care? We were not trying to get through the math, but were trying to get the math through him! The end of the story is that I saw his dad a few days ago. This young man is in a prestigious college and has a 3.9 GPA these days. Yes, he built the skill of overcoming problems. That's the name of the game for us in educating our students. We teach them to endure, stay patient, and keep seeking to get better rather than comparing themselves to others. It's the Skills Acquisition Mindset that often makes the difference.

Chapter 6

Teaching Mindset 3: The Parenting Aim

Grow a Happy Adult

Aiming to grow a happy adult is the least obvious of all the mindsets. I say it's the least obvious because we are all so prone to think in terms of the next moment rather than in terms of the years ahead. Loving-but-shortsighted parents can easily interfere with the growth and preparation of their independent students.

Let me begin by admitting that I struggled as an overweight child. I wore 'huskies', which meant I was sort of as wide as I was tall! I only mention this because it forced me to look at the long-term implications of short-term decisions, like ice cream. Once upon a time when our kids were small, we were having lunch with some good friends. After lunch, the ice cream came out and the mom was giving the kids giant scoops of the frozen drug. In her defense, her son went on to play college ball, so he could eat that much. I looked at her and said, "That's too much for our kids." I was probably blunt, but she and I had a great discussion. Specifically, I observed that the empty stomach is about the size of a closed fist. In that case, she was giving them 3 to 4 giant scoops, so about ten times the size of their stomach. I went a little further and said, "If this was proportional for adults, each person would be getting about a quart or two of ice cream." In that moment, she shot back the words that help me grasp this the most lastingly, "Why don't you want your kids to be happy?"

Happy kids – isn't that what we all really want? I think as parents and teachers that is a driver, but it is easy for us to get misled. I believe the unspoken theory is that happy kids lead to happy adults. Unfortunately, that is just psychobabble, a theory that sounds good until it is investigated. It's also incredibly dangerous when it comes to education, since most kids aren't exactly 'happy' when they are doing schoolwork. As one of my mentors likes to say, "Happiness isn't a constant state, it's just a place you visit." Empowering students to direct their own lives is the best gift we can give them, and that comes by teaching them to overcome problems and challenges. I'm convinced that the more we solve problems for them, the more dependent they become on us to solve their problems. Sadly, this usually turns into resentment.

Think for a moment about a couple of questions:

1. Just because you have a happy childhood, why does that mean you will be a happy adult?

2. Just because you have an unhappy childhood, why does that mean you will be an unhappy adult?

The answer to both is that, "It doesn't." We actually can spoil a child and set them on a course of misery by doing too much for them. As Dr. Hendricks used to say in class at Dallas Seminary, "If you keep doing something for someone they can do themselves, you'll turn them into a cripple." In principle, that turns out to be true indeed. We all understand about abuse and the horrors it can produce. But, there are also amazing stories about the abused turning out to be amazing examples of grace and courage. I'm not advocating abuse at all, but I am saying human resilience can overcome.

Happiness is not about a lifetime; rather it is about a moment. A good childhood doesn't really guarantee anything if you don't keep thinking well and acting noble. Perhaps what you do in a life adds up to a lifetime, but when we think about what-causes-what it is about the now and not the past.

Imagine how trapped anyone would feel if they thought, "My childhood was so unhappy I can never (ever) find happiness." It would be hopeless, and it would be untrue. The same might happen for someone who simply is confused because life is challenging as an adult, although childhood was happy and worry free.

The real aim is to grow happy adults. Happy adults come from well equipped children, children who are emotionally balanced and know how to solve their own problems and reach their own goals. Parenting, at its heart, is really mentoring. When you mentor someone, you are not trying to get them happy (or happy with you). Instead, you are attempting to get them ready. It reminds me of the scout motto: Be Prepared. Baden-Powell, the founder of scouting was asked one time, "Be prepared for what?" His response was, "For any old thing!" That is the idea, and we are to focus on preparing them so they can be happy adults. This long term orientation is a significant part of the proper mindset. If we just want to keep our kids home and parent them until we die (they never leave), then we are doing them a great disservice. Frankly, underneath this kind of well meant dysfunction is the faulty aim of seeking to grow happy kids rather than happy adults. Of course, if you can pull off both, then more power to you! Then again, never sacrifice a prepared-and-happy-adult for a momentarily happy child. The easiest way to say this is simply to assert that happy adults who can do math were once unhappy kids doing math problems!

Chapter 7

Teaching Mindset 4: The Educational Aim

Grow a Self-Teaching, Independent, Learner

What do you think about teaching? What's your philosophy? How do you think it works? Even though the title of this section is clear, it is most likely that you do not understand the radical idea presented or the various ways in which it can change everything for your homeschool.

Quickly, however, we must begin with a little logic to understand what's up here. Formal logic is largely about a premise(s) and a conclusion, and commonly has some kind of 'If…then' framework.

Premise – a proposition which supports a conclusion

Conclusion – a final opinion based a proposition

Well, that may not seem helpful, and there's a lot more going on, but it does fairly represent how we get to what we all do, suggest, or demand. Knowing that this is the way our minds work is a great help. And yes, I am dismissing that we are all emotionally driven and make decisions based on emotions. I get it that you want something before you buy it, but there still is a 'logic' beneath the emotions; it's unavoidable. Even the studies that 'prove' we are irrational admit that underneath the crazy choices we sometimes make are our own perceptions and application of experiences, so that what we do 'makes sense' in the moment from our frame.

Let's consider an example. Actually, anything you do has this basic structure behind it. If you believe abortion is right, then you have something like this in play—

If (premise) a woman has the right to control her own body,

> **Then** (conclusion) she has the right to remove a fetus from her body.

If you believe abortion is WRONG, then you have something like this in play—

If (premise) a fetus is a unique human baby who has a right to live,

> **Then** (conclusion) no one (not even the mother) has the right to kill a unique human baby.

That's a religious and political hot potato, so maybe something a little less inflammatory might help. My daughter Laura, when she was around eleven years old, stopped eating meat of any kind. While she said it was just that she didn't like it, I assumed there was something more in play. We didn't make a big deal of it, but we were concerned since we've had friends and families who have struggled with eating disorders of various types. One day Laura came into my office with her bible and showed me a passage from Genesis that she asserted said, "We were made to eat vegetables only." Of course, I knew more from the bible that I could show her, but first I wanted to understand her logic. As we continued to talk about it, she finally got it out in the open that she believed that animals had souls (thanks Bambi / Disney). From there she thought that if she didn't eat meat, then she was saving animals from death. Her logic looked like this—

If (premise) animals have souls like humans,

Then (conclusion) killing them is like murdering humans.

AND

If (premise) I don't eat meat,

Then (conclusion) some animals won't be murdered to feed me.

While there are a number of premises/conclusions involved that aren't mentioned, these two were the basics. A change in either conclusion would change everything. A change in one premise would also change everything. Once I knew this I showed her from the bible (since she saw it as authoritative) that Noah was told it's OK to eat animals for food (Genesis 9:3), that Peter was told it's OK to eat animals (Acts 10:9-16), and that Jesus himself ate fish and even cooked them for his disciples (John 21:9).

At that moment her opinion or conclusion changed. The very next day she began to eat meat again (sparingly) and has never looked back. The truth is that we take actions based on our assumptions and conclusions. Whether or not we should eat meat as a matter of science and health is another question, since I am pretty much a plant-based person myself (for my heart-health). The problem comes about when we are unthinkingly compelled to do things because of our unexamined logic.

Now, how does this relate to education? It's rather simple. If you think students must be taught, then you'll go in one direction. If you think students best learn by teaching themselves, then you'll go in another direction.

If (premise) children must be taught to learn,

Then (conclusion) we must provide teachers for our children.

It makes perfect sense that we have to find a school, a tutor, or a great curriculum if our children are to learn; at least, it makes perfect sense if the above is true. Next, we multiply the challenge with another bit of logic:

If (premise[1]) a teacher must know the subject in order to teach it;

...AND...

If (premise[2]) a student can only learn from someone who knows the subject better than they themselves know it;

Then (conclusion) a homeschool teacher (usually a mom) must be more
knowledgeable than her child.

If this is followed as what makes sense, then moms must study a lot to keep ahead of their kids. Moreover, there comes a point where the child must go to school somewhere because they are passing mom's skill level in one or more subjects. How painful, time-consuming, and somewhat failing this can become. True?

How about an entirely different logic? What might happen if this was not the way to think?

In our experience, it is the goal itself that should help inform our logic. We believe the goal is for everyone to become a self-teacher. All education eventually gets down to the student teaching himself. You might also think of the endgame of education as learning how to learn.

If (premise[1]) a teacher can help (but can't force) a student to learn a subject

AND

If (premise[2]) learning is the responsibility of the student

AND

If (premise[3]) people tend to agree (work well) with themselves
Then (conclusion) the student's best option is to become her own teacher

Now, from the student's view, he is empowered to realize that he is in control of his own learning. Once anyone gets that learning is within their own control, then the future is in their own hands. Independence comes when one's learning is no longer dependent on someone or something outside; that's the essence of being an independent learner.

Chapter 8

Teaching Mindset 5: The Management Aim

Be the CLO of Your Homeschool

Some time ago I read a book about management that discussed the various mistakes managers make. The very first principle was listed as the mistake of seeking to change actions instead of thinking. It's really an excellent point, and so often we see managers railing against what people are doing without helping them first understand how to think. The thinking issue is really about intention as much as it is anything else. If you are the 'manager' of your homeschool, then you need to be careful about your aim. Some parents function as though their aim is to be the Chief Record-keeping Officer (CRO). Others seem to be focus on being the CFO, or Chief Fun Officer. Well, you get the drift.

My plea is to invite you to become the Chief Learning Officer. In this role you are focused NOT on teaching, but rather on causing your students to learn. This may seem like a minor distinction, but it is not at all. Aiming at causing your student to learn helps you grow him as his own teacher. Aiming at 'teaching' helps him grow as a dependent student. Of course, I'm not concerned here about early elementary aged kids or younger. I'm talking about your orientation and direction for your students by the time they leave your home.

Are you focused on helping them grow as learners who can self-teach, or are you focused on having to learn everything yourself first so you can teach them? That's the rub, and that's the place for victory. Make a decision that your role is to cause them to learn, to create an environment for their development as those who can think and learn independently. Make a decision to become the CLO, the Chief Learning Officer of your homeschool. I promise, you'll never regret it.

SECTION III

THE 5 KEYS FOR A SUCCESSFUL INDEPENDENT HOMESCHOOL

Chapter 9

Key 1: The Magic of Mental Models

You can find a lot of information out there about mental models, especially if you are in the business world and read works that originate from the Sloan School of Management (MIT). You can't, however, find much about it applied to homeschooling. What I am about to share with you is almost magic and has amazing applications to business, organizations, and government. And yet, because I think the family is the most leveraged organization in a society, I want to focus here, for you. I also want you to understand that while there is a vibrant conversation about these things, I don't know of anyone who has been able to put it together like I have been privileged to do. As wild as it sounds, and I know that some of what I'm sharing will sound like many others, I believe God actually wired me together and guided me carefully to these insights. As you'll see in the words ahead, the most strategic thing to know is that a Mental Model is actually a combination of what I'll call Story (Fiction) and Strategy. To my knowledge, no one has explained Mental Models this way, in this combination. I believe it will transform your homeschool and the education of your own children more than anything else. We will discuss this a bit more with The Other Great Pyramid (just ahead), but for now just hold the thought that I'm about to give you fire!

Do you know the story of Prometheus? In Greek mythology, he was the one who defied the gods and gave fire to mankind. Fire, of course, was the basis of the growth of civilization because it uniquely allowed for the creative shaping of metal into tools, instruments, etc. His punishment was to be bound to a rock and have his liver eaten by an eagle. His liver grew back daily to be eaten again. Personally, I like the version where he was finally rescued by Hercules! Basically, Prometheus was a champion of human creativity and advancement. The liver was thought of as the seat of the emotions. So, it seems creativity and advancement were under attack by a threatened Zeus.

I mention this because that's exactly what I'm seeking to do. I want to give you the 'fire of the gods' so you can advance your own home and learning environment. Learning to work with mental models in the simplest of ways is plenty to transform your life.

You can begin with noticing that your very thought at hand sets in motion the actions that make sense to match the thought. Basically, thoughts and actions like to match. If you think I'm offering something of great value to you (and I am), then you'll keep reading and wrestling through the concepts I'm offering. If you think you already know all this stuff, then you'll be off to the next shiny object to help you along. It doesn't matter to me, but it is important to understand that the way you think things work makes all the difference in the world.

Ideas have consequences. That's the trick. That's the thing. When you get a clear-and-fresh idea, it can change everything.

When you strategically help your students get a clear-and-fresh idea, it can change everything for them as well, true?

Imagination Work vs. Reality Work

We grossly underplay the importance of this slight distinction, but it doesn't negate its importance. All of the work we do as humans is either in the domain of the imagination or it is in the domain of reality. The unfortunate thing, especially in America, is that our pragmatism underplays the importance of the imagination. I can't recount the number of times those I've coached or counseled have mentioned how they were shamed by the family for day-dreaming and reading. What we seem to forget is that every building needs an architect. There is simply no good way to build anything without one of those folks! Yes, and if someone doesn't build it, then the plans wouldn't matter. Ah, true but mis-emphasized! It is the plan for the house or factory or rocket or dress that gives rise to the making of that dress. A solid plan for educating our kids and growing independent learners simply MUST precede the work we do in the real world of education.

Here's an experiment to see the power of this point. Take 15 minutes a day for one week to imagine and plan what you hope to accomplish in your day ahead. This is the imagination work part. Next, go give it a try based on your imagination work. You might fail, but so what? Actually try it for five days and see if you don't accomplish more, find more achievement, and see more happiness in what gets done. In any project or sport or vacation, the planning and strategizing of the imagination before acting will make the work in reality massively more effective and focused. Honestly, just getting a husband to actually plan an evening out can change everything…well, you get my point.

NEVER EXPECT THINGS TO TURN OUT WELL WITHOUT A PLAN

I'm not sure how to make it clearer for you, but that's the power of imagination work. That is exactly what having a plan or strategy is all about. Reading a book by starting with the first word and moving to the second word, etc., is a plan for reading that affects how you read. Another plan is to survey the book first; looking at the table of contents, the back cover, thumbing through and reading a little randomly (especially the ends of chapters). Next, the book is read word-by-word. This second strategy is far more effective for understanding and learning the information. It takes a few minutes longer at first, but the time it saves is almost boundless.

That's the story behind mental models and almost everything you do in life, especially in your homeschooling efforts. You have a way you think about it and a strategy that matches it. If you think children are naturally good learners, then you might make things more casual throughout the day; giving kids room to explore and learn. If you think kids are more prone to watch TV and eat nothing but ice cream, then you'll likely have a matching strategy for getting a different set of habits and interests into their souls.

Of course, this is why the imagination work is so vital to what you do. The plan actually comes from how you think about anything. If you think you can't figure out how to homeschool, then you'll buy a weighty curriculum, hire tutors, or send them back to some kind of school. Coops and study groups (I'm thinking Classical Conversations on the extreme), are good examples of 'homeschool' that isn't really homeschool. I like to stress the fact that I love all education if it works, so I'm certainly a fan of CC and other group learning adventures. I do believe that all learning eventually comes down to the individual, so I am also a big fan of cultivating independence. I also notice know that parents often stress out over the work required on the part of the parent to help the kids keep up with the group. Sometimes this kind of competition helps and sometimes it hurts. As you'll see later, much of this comes down to clarity concerning your idea of success in homeschool.

In summary — we think, then we plan. That's all there is to it, so where do you start? You start with the thinking part, and I promise, most parents are drifting in a sea of assumptions, half-truths, and clichés. Imagination work is actual work, and the actual work that makes the biggest long-term difference. There is an easier way to start clarifying your thinking so you can clarify your plan. I call it the Other Great Pyramid and it explains almost everything about getting results in this life.

The Other Great Pyramid

I have spent a lifetime returning to the question, "How do we get results?" It might take different forms such as, "How do we create? How do we solve problems? How do we get more productive?" Nonetheless, I've always been stretching to understand exactly why we take the actions we take to get the results we get. Of course, the issue isn't really about getting the results we want, it's about getting the results we don't want. I've thought about this a great deal and it appears that most of us, most of the time, aren't really getting the outcomes we hope. In your own homeschool setting, are the kids (in their learning, their virtue, their actions, their focus, their attitude, etc.) doing just how you'd imagine? Probably not, unless you have no aspirations or hopes at all for your children. All of this leads to the other Great Pyramid, which is my own version of how to understand how we humans produce (and fail to produce) results.

So, here's the picture of The Other Great Pyramid © Fred Ray Lybrand Jr., 2013

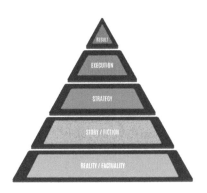

Reality – This is the domain of what is, what is actual, what is factual. While it is common to understand perception as reality, I like to observe that misperception is reality too. What we are concerned with is the actual information, the data, the what is 'true' concerning anything we are interested in related to the results we desire. It could also be called factuality.

Story – This is the place perception and misperception actually belong. This is the domain where we try to make sense of the facts that are relevant to our endeavor. I like to think of it as fiction because it allows me a little more freedom to reconsider how I'm trying to make sense of the facts I'm looking at. Technically, story/fiction may belong on the bottom, serving as the filter that defines the facts we see. In either case, the two bottom parts interact on the way to strategy.

Strategy – This is the plan that is birthed from our understanding of the facts through our story. A strategy is all about how you will approach getting the results you want.

Execution – This is the action level of implementing or doing our strategy. Execution may be poor or excellent, but it alone produces the results we see within the boundaries of what we can control. Of course, though it alone produces results because it is the point of action; it is utterly dependent on the Reality-Story-Strategy that gives it direction.

Results – This is what happens from the actions taken in the execution stage. The results may be what you want, or maybe they are close-but-need-adjustments. Adjustments are part of the Reality-Story-Strategy-Execution; if they are missing, then it's because of what's going on in the rest of the pyramid. In the overall use of the Pyramid to adjust any area of life, it is almost always best to begin with the results. Learn to ask, "What do I want?" Or, "What would make me happy to create?"

By now you probably are seeing that these things are essentially a system and cannot easily be separated from one another.

How it Works – The Other Great Pyramid is my way of thinking about how our thinking affects our actions, and how the principle of alignment needs to be in play in our quest to produce results. If you think about it, it's just a logical move from facts to results by understanding that we interpret the facts (using story) and make a plan (strategy) based on the story that we act upon (execution) so results happen. There is really not much more to it; except, we need to admit we can be confused by hypotheticals. A hypothetical is basically a theory used to guess at outcomes. If they are wildly speculative, we'll just get confused. When we are confused, we design plans that won't work. When we are hypocrites, we simply don't act with the story. If you are thinking clearly, then you'll realize that The Other Great Pyramid offers you control over your life. You now have a map with which to understand why you don't (and do) get the result you want in life. Of course, we all know that time and chance happen to us all, but there is still how we act and react that influences the happenstance of our lives in small and great ways.

The Other Great Pyramid works by each level being built on the one below it, while at the same time having the level above confirming and influencing the level below. Here's a way to picture it:

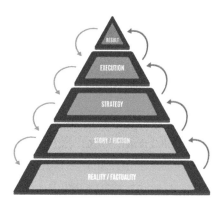

You can imagine this works from bottom to top to bottom, but it also works between any two levels that are touching. So, you might realize that you can't execute a plan because of time or money constraints. As a result, you adjust the strategy because of the influence of the execution issue. It also can work the other way as well; your strategy can influence ways to execute that you never had thought or considered. When Jody and I concluded we wanted to spend less time teaching the kids and more time encouraging them to teach themselves, we realized that we didn't need to grade math because the kids could check each other's math. The same conclusion came about to have the kids debrief among themselves what they had read that day. Having the students take on the math corrections and reading review made everything much simpler.

An added bonus was that the kids all became more vigilant in holding one another accountable. Again, this pyramid might more commonly work with the Story/Fiction at the bottom. I'm not confident people can really start with Reality/Facts; something else is probably always setting the context in our minds. So, we look at reality through a lens, at least at first.

How We Fail

If you haven't already realized it, we fail because we aren't adequately careful with each level in The Other Great Pyramid. If you miss some facts, then your story will be off. If your story is off, then your strategy will be headed in the wrong direction. If you execute well on a bad strategy, then your results will be predictably NOT what you wanted! Clearly, we can also simply neglect one of the levels. If we don't spend much energy on developing a strategy, then we'll probably just fly by the seat of our pants; which rarely produces the results we want. Having a plan for teaching a child to read works better than having no 'real' plan except to read to them a lot. Oddly enough, the second plan can work okay for about 20 percent of students. Nonetheless, that 20 percent can learn with a reading (think phonics) curriculum too. So, a good reading plan works for virtually everyone. [P.S. As an aside, I see that we are in a world that is busy insisting that we all should do things our own way because all our kids are unique. While that is true, it's not all that's true. In such things as swimming or tennis, we don't really create unique training systems for each person. Instead, students have to learn the basics before adjusting their 'game' to their own style. I see this mistake a lot in home education; we are sometimes using our child's uniqueness and our rights to 'parent and teach our own way' to accidentally harm our children. Instead, it is better to have them enjoy some discipline to learn the skills they need for life. It's similar to having them read the 'classics' to ground their knowledge and skill. Later on they can read whatever tripe they want to in adulthood, true? Most kids don't love-love reading all the classics, but so what?]

What is the Most Important Part of The Other Great Pyramid? Here you want to think - It's Leverage!

Ockham's Lever and The Other Great Pyramid

We know that every level of the Pyramid is important, however, since we have learned about leverage we can ask an important kind of question. Where is the leverage in the Great Pyramid? What one area of focus will make the biggest difference? Honestly, the answer is two-fold; technically and practically.

1.Technically the leverage is in the FACTS

The facts level of the pyramid really has the most powerful immediate influence. If a fact gets through to the story, then the story will change. It happens in the criminal world, archeology, and legitimate debates. A fact that simply won't go away must make the story adjust (or someone will hide, suppress, or distort the fact if they 'must' keep the story).

2.Practically the leverage is in the STORY

The story contains the most leverage for a couple of reasons. Remember, the story can also be fiction; the thing we 'make up' in order to explain the fact relevant to the thing we want (results). When we buy something costly, we commonly want it first and create a rationale (story) second.

The first reason there is more practical leverage in the story is that we can simply change the story. The easiest way I have found to change a story about anything is to come up with two additional possible explanations. In homeschooling, sometimes we have kids that aren't motivated to do their work. We could call that lazy and have a clear story that explains what we see in the child. But couldn't it be something else? Perhaps it's that the child is simply unchallenged because too little is demanded of him? Another option is that he's simply out-of-shape because he isn't outside doing some hard work or exercise on a daily basis. At any rate, you can suddenly see that the first version may not be true, so it's back to the facts to figure out what's really going on.

The second reason the story has the leverage is that it, whatever IT is, creates a grid or filter or sieve through which we receive and dismiss facts. When someone thinks homeschooling is 'evil', then they will simply look for information to support their viewpoint; certain studies will take precedence over other studies (which will be ignored). We see this commonly in media, politics, and religion. The other side is 100% wrong and so they are totally dismissed as biased. All the while, we are 100% dismissing them as well.

The leverage is in the story such that it helps us see facts we need to see, even as the facts help us form our story. Learning to improve your story will allow you to improve what you really see. This 'really seeing' is basically truth-telling, and is vital for the educated independent mind.

Finally, you can also substitute the word 'conclusion' for story. In effect, a conclusion we have about something is a story we believe. A group of conclusions form a full story. This story in turn helps us come up with a strategy, then we execute, then we get results. If you want to change the results you're getting in business or marriage or friendships or homeschooling, then you'll want to start working on the story. Begin by coming up with two more explanations. Next, look for some other facts that you may have overlooked. That's enough for you to start learning how to use the Other Great Pyramid. Visually speaking, here's where we focus (frankly, these are so entangled that it might be better to put the Story/Fiction at the base, emphasizing how we start with our story to see the details of Reality/Factuality):

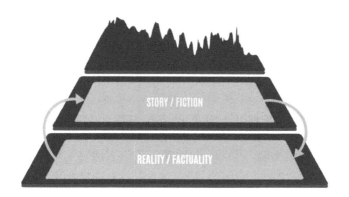

So What?

What do we do with this fresh way to think about how the story influences the results and outcomes we experience in life? Basically, our actions and approaches will be dramatically influenced by our story; that's the essence. If you underestimate this reality and insist that you are acting without regard to a story, then you'll function more like a robot than a human being (was that too harsh?). We can't do much about executing on our plans, but we can do a lot about the facts we uncover and the way we interpret them.

In education, for example, we have a couple of basic ways to look at our homeschool students and what is going on in the learning process. The first approach is also the most common these days and is formally called the Tabula Rasa or 'blank slate'. The idea is that students are like chalkboards or whiteboards and have nothing written upon them, they are blank. The role of the teacher is clearly to 'write stuff' on the student's mind. I believe this philosophy motivates a lot of indoctrination, since people believe that if they don't indoctrinate the student, others in the world will (with the wrong stuff). While I wouldn't deny that new stuff is written on the student's mind, I see this as terribly unempowering for the student. They become helpless learning victims in desperate need of someone to teach them. There is no real way this Tabula Rosa story leads to self-teaching.

The alternate model follows from the word for education in Latin, educare. When the word is dissected, it roughly means e (out) + duc (to lead or draw). In this view, education is the drawing out of what's already 'in' the student. In the Greek and Roman understanding, students had access to vast knowledge that was already embedded in, or access to, the human psyche. This story leads us on more of a path of self-discovery and personal responsibility. In 'educare' we see the foundation for the Socratic Method, but also employed by many great teachers, including Jesus of Nazareth. The notion behind the method was actually to help the tutor learn and discover more. However, the pupils benefitted as well, since everyone discussed the topic and made connections. It was as though everyone had a connection to vast knowledge, but something needed to trigger it. Of course, the Socratic Method produced Socrates, then Plato, then Aristotle, who tutored Alexander the Great. All of this was in Athens, a city of about 100,000, and none of these individuals were kin to one another! The story produced an educational approach that produced great thinkers.

Both of these views, Tabula Rasa and _educare_, are simply stories, but they inform our strategy, which affects our results.

What about you as a homeschooling family? What do you think about education? What is your story? For us it was all about helping the kids learn how to learn...that's all we really cared about. For us, this came down to a simple distinction that separated us from the public and private mass education alternatives; Skill vs. Socialization.

1. Socialization is an approach that sees the purpose of education as 'fitting' a student for the world in which she

will live. It is heavy on ideology and heavy on information. This preparation is largely a type of social engineering that confuses knowing a lot of stuff with being able to use what you know. It honestly doesn't easily match independent thought. Most people don't see it as socialization, but rather as 'busy work' or something like that. It is preparation to be a factory worker (even if the 'white collar' factory is putting out information and data rather than 'blue collar' nuts and bolts). It is preparation to win the daily double on Jeopardy. This is not the kind of equipping that real learners and real independent thinkers benefit from, though some are able to wade through this approach to a new place. Sadly, most people just learn to hate school and learning and reading…to finally arrive at needing to be told or shown what to do to keep their job.

2. Skill is an approach that sees the purpose of education as being trained to become a self-sufficient and adaptable learner. Remember Alfred North Whitehead's observation that, ""Education is the acquisition of the art of the utilization of knowledge." Education is the art of utilizing, or using, knowledge. This orientation is quite different and follows the old adage about giving a man a fish vs. teaching a man to fish. One feeds him for a day. The other for a lifetime. That is it exactly; we want a story that helps us grow students who will learn for a lifetime. Lifetime learners are skilled learners. They may not know how to do something, but they can figure it out, study it, or find someone who can help them catch

on quickly. A skilled person is one who is truly independent, one who is ready for a variety of career changes that will naturally occur in our present job climate.

What are these skills? Well, there are ten skills we believe are necessary for independent learning. You might find others that are helpful, but we aim for 'enough' to be on the life-long path of learning. Just to be clear, there are really just three essential skills required for all effective learning as humans for our 'modern' world; reading, writing, and arithmetic. They may sound familiar as the 3R's, but know they are the essentials which gave birth to the cliché. Reading as a skill gives you access to the great minds of history (or for anything you'd like to learn). Math is the language of science and gives you training in logic and causality and absolutes (all of which are quite handy to develop wisdom and effective problem-solving skills). Finally, writing is the hardest of the skills because it demands the clearest of thoughts in order to effectively convey information to others.

Imagine how your homeschool will change if you shift from a 'pile up knowledge' story to an 'add skills to their toolbox' story. You will quit competing with the mass education systems which just pretend that knowing stuff is what counts. Instead, you will compete with you student's current skill level compared to the next level to achieve. Knowing Algebra I is compared with knowing Algebra II. Comparison to others isn't the focus for education with this story. In fact, it's more like golf; you made par on one hole today, but can we figure out how to make a birdy tomorrow?

The 10 Skill Areas of Independent Learning

Over the years of work with children and adults as an educator, pastor, author, and communicator, I settled on ten basic skill areas everyone needs to do well in this world. I'm sure we could add more to the list (or even reduce it to an essential three or four), but I'd simply say, "This is plenty." Each of these skills impact other related ones, so you can see that these cluster around learning and communication and thinking and problem-solving. A simple test to appreciate the value of each is to remove it as a skill from your student in her imaginary future. What's she like if she can't write? How does she do if she is simply deficient in relating to others? You get the point. A person who is adequately skilled in these areas is a person who should do just fine in life. Yes, there is plenty more concerning morality and spirituality, but from a skill-set viewpoint in our mental model we should be on target. This is imagination work to begin pursuing. Think about your own students, or kids, or grandkids (or your nation) as you consider these areas. What will they be like if they master each of these?

Emotions – This area is about learning how to run one's own emotions. It is quite striking how increasingly irresponsible our society seems to label the next generation. Of course, I don't see that much clarity on this topic in my generation either. Imagine if your student could get himself un-upset without your help or anyone else's? What if he didn't 'feel' like doing something, but knew how to change the way he thinks-and-feels so as to get on with what needs to be done? That's why this area is so vital. It would be something to teach all kids more about how to run their emotions; perhaps it would cut back on crime and killings in our nation's schools and streets?

Goals – While the importance of this area doesn't go without saying, it probably should. Understanding how to clarify and objective or aim in life is a valuable and big deal. We all talk about dreams and 'what do you want to be' to our kids, but rarely do we help them understand a solid process for how to pursue what they want in life. Most kids are waiting for someone to tell them what to do so they can do it (or rebel). Mastering goal-setting is one of those skills that every child needs to learn for effectiveness for the rest of his life.

Focus - Focus is a growing problem in our society. Not only is there the great ADHD debate and the use of drugs, as a cure there is also simply the overwhelm of our phones and computers and televisions constantly interrupting our focus. Fortunately, focus is a skill that can be developed in almost anyone. Similar to running in that we are not all race winning marathoners, most of us can still run okay. Focus is much the same; perhaps there are a few Olympians of focus, but we can all learn the skill well enough to aid us in life success.

Memory – While this area is a bit of a 'duh' in most of our minds, there is so much we can do to enhance our ability to use and grow our faculty for memory. Mere memory work is great up until about ten years old, but after that it isn't the best part of education. On the other hand, learning every subject requires the engagement of a good memory. A good memory can just appear for a lucky few, but most need a little help learning how to run this part of their brain as a skill for life.

Time – Often people don't really think of this as a legitimate area of skill development for students, but what has more direct impact? I watch parents all over the nation constantly serve as timekeepers and assistants to their own kids. What could develop more dependence and irresponsibility than that? Imagine a student owning how time and actions relate such that she can organize her day - week - month to accomplish what she wants or needs to get done?

Reading – Reading is the most essential skill for independent learning. Think about what reading offers us. With reading we can tap into the greatest minds in history, whether they are dead or alive. With reading we can access the information necessary to learn anything. On top of it all, plenty of studies demonstrate that reading actually improves the brain itself (vs. television). The great mistake with reading is that we often don't help our students learn how to look at the whole before looking at the individual words, which in turn makes reading tedious and unrewarding. We also leave out the idea that reading is a bridge to something and not an end in itself. Imagine if your student caught fire because she knew reading could get her closer to everything she wants in life. This is exactly why reading needs to be a skill our students learn to love.

Writing – It is common for people to think math is the most difficult subject, but math is easy compared to writing. The only thing that makes math difficult is that we are thrown new concepts with each math lesson. If you did the same lesson daily, then you'd be bored in no time. Writing, on the other hand, is very challenging. Besides our great fears about others reading our writing and thinking something awful about us, writing is complicated. When we write a mere paragraph or two, we are engaged in making hundreds of decisions about word choice, punctuation, grammar, etc. Writing really is about thinking. When we write we are forced to think with greater clarity. Immediately this leads to writing as valuable for communication, true? Getting someone to think as you think is the aim of communication. Fortunately we have an instinct for language, so the opportunity is just ahead for your student (no matter where he is now).

Problem-Solving – Problem- solving is clearly related to math, but it is also about so much more. A math problem has a few variables and a sequence to 'solve' the problem. Life often functions the same way. We encounter an obstacle, we see a few variables, we think about a sequence of steps, and tada!...problem solved! Of course, it doesn't always go that way, but if we really teach our students how to hone the skill of problem-solving, then life gets incredibly less difficult and painful for them. Life is loaded with problems, so why wouldn't this be a premier skill for our students to learn on the path toward independence? Frankly, the reason we are hired for a job is because we solve problems for our employer.

Communication – Using the information we learn by reading and writing and problem-solving comes down to communication. Why? Since we are social beings and accomplish things with others, then in order for our knowledge to become useful it must be understood by others. Weakness as a communicator interferes with work, love, impact, and even placing an order at Chick-fil-A. We simply must learn to communicate effectively to function well as independent learners who touch the world.

Relationships – Finally, almost everything comes down to relationships; friends, family, marriage, and helping strangers is all relational. Sadly, relationship success is one of the great weaknesses with humans. We develop enemies along the way as well, largely from not knowing how to patch things up. However, even more importantly, we don't seem to know how to find and grow the right friendships. The skill of befriending others, whether at work or play, is a strategic skill for any independent learner.

The "Easier in Theory Than in Practice" Error

This particular mental model will kill your success before you get started, and for the simple reason that it is usually employed as an excuse. An excuse for what? An excuse for failure, certainly. But more venomous is that we can use it as an excuse to avoid trying. We tend to think something is easier in practice than in theory because it's easy to come up with a theory because people do it all the time. Proving the theory in reality is another story. Okay, I'll admit that a shoddy theory is easier to invent than it is to put it into the real world, but that's only because it won't work in the real world. Instead, I'm suggesting that you take the thinking work even more seriously. If you have a theory that works, then you can be sure the results can happen as well. Einstein and his view of the relationship between energy and matter unleashed all kinds of results by clearly lesser minds. Tesla's view of Alternating Current won out eventually over Edison's insistence on Direct Current. The list is endless, because results begin with the idea being worked out in someone's head. Yes, happy accidents happen (see Reese's Peanut Butter Cup commercials), but we really don't want to rely on them, do we?

Basically, this gets back to the importance of imagination work. Consider the following,

My method is different. I do not rush into actual work. When I get a new idea, I start at once building it up in my imagination, and make improvements and operate the device in my mind. When I have gone so far as to embody everything in my invention, every possible improvement I can think of, and when I see no fault anywhere, I put into concrete form the final product of my brain. —Nikola Tesla

So, quit pitting theory and practice against one another and get down to the business of really thinking through your homeschool aims and practices before you start. Spend some time picturing what a day will look like, how you will handle struggles, and what your student's final transcript will look like. I'm talking about some hard thinking that will pay off handsomely. In fact, once you've got the idea worked out well, the execution of the plan can often feel like fun rather than painfully hard work.

For a quick taste-and-see, pause reading and think about the following for three minutes:

What would it look like in our homeschool if the kids all figured out things for themselves? What problems would we face in getting them there? How could we solve these problems?

Chapter 10

Key 2: Your System is Your Success

DEFINING THINGS. The simplest way to go in life is to figure out how life works, and then work it. In my experience, the most important insight is how causality works; that is how things happen. If you misunderstand how things happen, then you cannot reliably improve them. There's a Latin phrase for a logical fallacy: *Post hoc ergo propter hoc*, which means 'after this, therefore because of this'. It's a mistake we make in thinking that because something happened before something else happened, the first thing is the cause. I was first introduced to this idea in a speech class at the University of Alabama The professor shared that he had gone to a friend's house to stay and was using an old fashion bathroom that had neon lights on either side of a mirror. Well, he didn't know fluorescent lights took a moment to come on since they were new to him. As a result he would turn the switch on and nothing would happen, next he would tap on the tube which would then light up. His assumption was that his tapping the fluorescent tube made it come on. Imagine this fallacy with your own homeschooling and educational practices. It really doesn't matter if it's parenting, or sports, or even how you approach something as common as a video game, watching TV, or any number of the distractions we experience in this world. They all come down to one thing; they operate by systems. System thinking is an understanding of causality (the way things work) based on the combination of elements involved and how they affect one another. We tend to think in terms like A affects B, B affects C, and C affects D. Well, of course that can happen but for the most part in systems thinking, it's really that A affects B, B affects D, D affects C, C affects A, A affects C, C affects B, and B affects D, and it keeps going.

Weather systems are a great example. The weather is probably the most powerful way you can understand your homeschooling practice. What makes it rain? Think for a moment about that question. What makes it rain? We could say there's water in the air. We can say clouds make it rain. We can say it's the cooling and condensing process, you know, cooling so water condenses in the air. The fact of the matter is all these elements are necessary. You have to have adequate humidity, but even with adequate humidity you still need something to trigger the rain. Commonly we see this in the United States with cold fronts, (cold fronts are really just cool air relative to the warm air they are encountering. When cool air and warm moist air run into each other, in that context the system squeezes water out of the air onto the ground. In the heat of the South the same thing happens with day time heating-cooling cycles. So, it's common to see a thunderstorm in the afternoons in the summer. If there's enough moisture in the air, and daytime cooling occurs, those elements come together to create a storm.

Global warming or climate change, is another good example of understating causality. Basically, we're told that humans have put too much carbon in the air which creates a greenhouse type of effect, such that the overall temperature is changing on the planet. This change will have repercussions with seasons and storms and sea levels. Now, maybe that's true, but it's definitely A affects B, affects C, affects D type of thinking. It's not actually systems oriented, because in a systems orientation you don't talk about what one thing causes a result without talking about all the elements in play. Maybe indeed the carbon is affecting warming. It's also unclear if warming is a good thing or a bad thing. It certainly seems to me that the earth has been warming since the ice age and these cycles are a part of the whole nature of the system of the earth. Now, my point is not to get into the controversy of global warming, but to just understand that from a systems viewpoint, to be confident about this kind of complexity, holding that one element is having that kind of total effect on everything is, to say the very least, not very scientific.

In the 2016 election, when Trump became president, we could ask, "Why?" If we conclude it was because Trump tapped into the heartbeat of middle America, or because Hillary Clinton had a poor campaign, or because people stayed home and didn't vote, then we're caught up in misunderstand the nature of systems. It's the combination of things that makes the difference. Applying this to our homeschooling and educational efforts begins to make sense of everything for me, and I hope it does for you. What produces an educated, independent individual? Is it learning how to read and write and do mathematics? Is it learning self-discipline? Is it learning how to follow a routine? Is it learning how to not follow a routine, but be lateral and inventive in one's thinking? I'm very confident it is all of those things and much more because the nature of learning, and growing as a human being is a system. We need to realize there are a number of elements that affect each other. We can include things like personality, what is modeled, and what the environment exposes an individual to experience. How do we use this material or this understating of systems to help educate our children? In our experience, the two simplest things to use are processes and recipes. Processes and recipes are really processes and checklists. Processes and checklists are easy ways to set up systems. Some years ago two of our children were engaged in a fair bit of conflict. As a good dad I was trying to teach them to communicate. But everything I taught them to do in communication continued to intensify their conflict. So, I taught them about how to first understand and then be understood, how to explain the other person's viewpoint before you disagree. All that happened is that their conflict became worse and more exaggerated as they tried to communicate.

On a particularly balmy evening on vacation, in the central part of Alabama at Lake Martin, there was a particular conflict that reached into my heart and pulled out frustrations that I had not been aware that I had. I got really upset and spent some time thinking about it. In fact I woke up at 4 in the morning and sat out on the screened in porch and prayed and thought. As I prayed and thought, I first asked the question, "Was I too hard on the boys?" and God essentially said to me, "No, you were fine." Well, that was good to hear, but then I asked, "What do I do?" He said "I taught you all that stuff about systems and processes, why don't you use it?" So, at that moment I sat down and made up a process for the kids, and after I explained it to them and they acknowledged it, there was not another conflict for the next year and a half before one of them left for college. Imagine, simply having one list, that we placed on our refrigerator transformed the conflict in our home. Would you like to know the system? I'll get to that in a moment.

First think about what a process actually is, just a sequence of actions that lead to a particular result. So, in order or create a process all you need to do is think about the result you want, and then sort out the steps that will produce it. When we think of education, the very definition of how we think about education and the outcome we desire for our students, will dictate the process to us. In fact, that's the core thought of this entire book. We're just considering how to set up processes for the particular results we want. We wanted children who could be independent learners, who could teach themselves, so all of our processes were designed to encourage them to teach themselves. That was the secret to solving the communication issue. As I sat there on that back porch, I asked myself what I really wanted. What I really wanted, was for the kids to resolve their own conflicts without involving me or their mother. I wanted them to do it in a quiet way, or a way that didn't disrupt our home. Now, we happen to have 4 acres, so I told them they can certainly go to any boundary of our property and not bother the neighbors, or us if they get loud. In fact, I didn't care if they got loud. I just cared that they didn't get loud in the home. So, here's the essential plan:

Step 1. If a conflict that begins to happen, we'll give you a warning (because people can get animated in a moment, and that's okay).

Step 2. After the warning, if you resolve it yourselves without disturbing the home, then all is well.

Step 3. If you do not resolve it yourselves then you will immediately sit down and write a three-page essay entitled, "Why he is wrong and I am right."

Step 4. The essays will be read to the judge, which means either their mother or me, and the judge will declare a winner.

Step 5. The winner will be taken downtown to get a special dessert like Tiramisu or Tres Leches.

Step 6. The loser will do a project in the backyard, like fixing a stone wall or digging a hole. Now, that may all sound hard but it wasn't the complete story. And now to this day, so many years later, they never wrote a single essay and they never dug a single hole. The process was completed with a seventh step

Step 7. If you resolve all of your issues together without disturbing the home for one month, you'll get an entire day off from school. Since we homeschooled, and I was the headmaster, I could declare a free day for them; and that's what we did.

After five months we stopped the system and the conflicts started rising up again. So I said "Okay, I can't give you the free days off anymore, but we will keep the essays in place." From then on there was no problem. That's the nature of setting up a process. I always think of recipes in a similar way. A recipe is an amazing, thing because it allows us to do is take a top chef's dish and create a pretty close representation in our own kitchen. Imagine the power of that! You have a sequence of steps that you can follow that produce a result that you wouldn't have created by yourself. This actually goes to the issue of checklists. In the book, The *Checklist Manifesto*, the author explains how checklists became the safety factor for airplanes. If you know anything about private or commercial airplanes there's a massive checklist that is followed in order to ensure safety. It was developed because of the failure of the B-1 bomber when it was first tested with the best pilot in America and, in that test fly, it crashed and burned. The inventors of the B-1 bomber, the fans of it, knew that it wasn't that we needed a better pilot but rather they began to look at the system. And the system involved four engines that had to have gas mixed just right, gas and oil mixed just right. And as a result, that complexity created flaws and mistakes. This is a common thing with human beings. If there are too many complex things that can distract you, we can fail. In fact, the famous chefs in New York City all use their own recipes in a written form so they can look at where they are in the process. If you have just added tarragon, and someone drops a pot and causes a grease fire you can get distracted, return to the recipe and not remember. If you didn't have a recipe and were just doing it from your head, you wouldn't know, "Did I put the tarragon in or not?" and you might double up or leave it out. So, what happens with the recipe is it makes us approach perfection. As an aside, I would say we never want to really try to be perfect, it's not worth it, 98% is plenty good, and you get to the same A plus rate anyway. That is the nature of a recipe, it gives us the powerful ability to stabilize what we are doing. This is what they learned about the B-1 bomber. Once they created a checklist of what to do, this, this, this, this, this, everything tended to work fine. The airlines learned that this was important for emergencies too, so they have an emergency checklist to pull out when something happens. You check this thing, this thing, this thing, this thing, which allows human beings to be clear and exacting without a panic or distraction. I know it might sound too mechanical, but it's really not. Your homeschool, if it has processes, and checklists in it, will run incredibly efficiently.

In our own home school, we learned a simple process that had in our mind the kids being responsible for their own learning. Our process looked something like this: at 7:30am every morning, school would begin with the idea of ending around 12:30pm for lunch, with no more school for the rest of day. Yes, in a five-hour period we basically did all our education for all the years, for all of our children. There are some nuanced pieces however. For example, our kids could not begin school until everyone was at the table. So, as a result, the kids were all responsible to wake the other siblings and get them downstairs at the table. Second, we had a simple sequence of working from writing, to math, to reading. So, on any given day, the children were spending 2 hours in math, 2 hours in reading, and 1 hour in writing. Now, there were adjustments with some students being more efficient, there was also some physical exercise included, but for the most part that was the sequence. It was a process. In our minds the process worked from doing the most difficult thing first, which was writing; so, they were learning the discipline of doing something difficult. As an aside, writing is far more difficult than math because you are making hundreds of decisions throughout every written page. Math is only difficult because you are getting introduced to a new idea with each lesson. If you studied it, or let's say did the same problems every day, math would become very boring in no time at all. It's only challenging because there's something entirely new. Writing is challenging because it's engaging your whole person; your understanding of language and grammar and punctuation and what you are trying to say, along with emotions, logic, etc. So, writing is quite a cool skill that coordinates all the thinking in a child, especially as they age. That's the nature of systems and processes and recipes. You want to think about these things, not in terms of schedules and routines, but more in the flow of a sequence. So, we are thinking about what do we do in the early part of the day, then through the middle part of the day, and still in the afternoon. By the way, we actually had things in the afternoons too. Our kids played sports, did scouts, and took music and art lessons in addition to creative free time. Yes, there were things during the week that included away from home activities, but a lot of the time they could just go play in whatever way that was wholesome and decent. They found lots of things to do and lots of friends to do them with. Play was always a valuable part of the process as well.

In closing, you want to think about this issue of success in your homeschool system kind of like it's jazz music. I know a little about music, but I have had those who understand it well explain that jazz is a form that is set up a certain way. Inside of the form of jazz there are spaces for innovating, or 'Scat Singing' along with the other cool things Louis Armstrong always did. So, jazz is a fair way to think about what you are trying to do with your parenting system and your education system and maybe even your fun system. You set up a structure, a system, a sequence, a process, a recipe with the frame, but there's room for flexibility inside of it. You have basic things you're getting done to organize the story and then some room for the individual to emerge. I think that's what I also like about having our children write every day; writing is the form, you are putting words you are making up on paper. And yet, what each child wrote was entirely different as we gave them the freedom to craft a story, a description, or a letter to their grandmother. It didn't really matter; we just provided a context for our kids to express themselves and learn as they went along.

All of this boils down to the use of processes and checklists. Processes are steps that outline the sequence to be used to get to a certain result. Checklists are similar and a little easier. Checklists simply record the things that must be done for a result to happen. Either way works pretty well, though processes are the real endgame. Just note well, you do not have to have a process for everything, just for the next thing that you want to make a steady part of your life, homeschool, or family. You could also think of these things as recipes. You are forming a recipe for success in a particular area.

Chapter 11

Key 3: The Skill-Set for Success

One of the most strategic things anyone can discover about education is that it is best approached as the process of acquiring skills. This is obvious in the trades; an educated plumber or electrician is skilled at producing the results the trade demands. Through their apprenticeships they train the uneducated to become educated. They train them with the right skills and the right knowledge to be successful.

Education, as we understand it for schooling, should never simply be about piling up knowledge. Nor should it be about promoting certain social or philosophical positions. Sadly, at this moment the universities are in an obvious state of corruption, emphasizing radical agendas and minimizing free speech. Of course, this creates a boon for independent forms of education like homeschooling, but it kills the growth of keen thinking and progress. Knowledge, often found around busy-work, is often just an exercise in trivia contest preparation. Can you name the capitols of all the states in America? Can you name the number of the most unstable uranium molecule? How many people were on the Titanic during its deadly voyage? These kinds of questions might be fun to know, but having the answers isn't the end-game of educating. Knowing how to find and use the answers is a different story.

Education is best understood as having the skills that open and maintain a life of learning, no matter the situation. If your child can effectively teach herself what she wants to learn, then 'not knowing' something is simply a temporary state of affairs. If she wants to find out about uranium 235, then she can and will, if she is educated to be an independent learner.

If skills are essential for true education, then what are the essential skills of the educated independent learner? Yes, you can guess; it's the 3 R's.

Teaching the 3 R's

Reading, w**R**iting, and a**R**ithmetic were articulated as essentials around 1800, though there's a little debate about where it first appeared. Even Augustine's Confessions (circa 400 AD) describes these skills as the essentials of learning. Why are they so valuable? Frankly, the 3 R's unlock everything for the independent learner. Consider them in order of difficulty:

Reading

While reading is probably the easiest of skills to master, it is clearly the most important of the three essentials. Easiest does not mean easy, but it is attainable for almost all of us. Reading is probably misnamed and should instead be called something like 'comprehension'. We do combine the words into reading-comprehension, but that actually displays the problem. We can be able to read properly, but still have no idea what the passage means. Reading is found in the ability to convert the letters (symbols) into sounds which form words. Words, when structured together convey thoughts. Thoughts, however, are not always that clear. As a result, we can enjoy messages with double-meanings and humor. For example, Benjamin Franklin is purported to have said after signing the Declaration of Independence, "Gentlemen, we must all hang together or most assuredly we will all hang separately." The context and the person direct us to understand that he is saying that unity is protection because it puts victory in reach. Disunity is a path to defeat and hanging from the gallows for the king as rebels. A good phonics program will teach your child to 'read', but comprehending is another matter altogether. Here are a few comprehension ideas that you might find helpful:

- When reading, learn to replace "What does it mean to you?" with "What do you think the author means? What do you think the author is trying to say?" This is known as authorial intent. It's a big issue in politics, constitutional law, and interpreting the Bible. What did the framers of the Constitution intend? That informs us of the meaning. If we ask, "What could this mean?" or "What does this mean to me?" then we are in the shaky world of imposing meaning on what is written, rather than deriving meaning. Comprehension is all about understanding what the sentences are trying to communicate, never about the reader telling the sentences what they 'should' mean by what they say.

- Separate "What does it say?" from "What does it mean?" This works along with the point above. In reading-comprehension, we are better off realizing that reading is one thing and understanding is something else. Of course, it's always about understanding, true?

- Look for patterns in what you are reading. A pattern is like the picture you see when a jigsaw puzzle is completed. There are various pieces that fit together in an understandable way. When these pieces come together, the first thing you commonly have is a rectangle. However, on the rectangle you have a picture of something. It is very much the same with patterns in what you read. When you can discern the pattern, you can quickly see and remember an enormous amount of information. A common pattern in a story is Tension-Resolution, or what you might think of as hinting. Tension-Resolution is a device used to create the sense of everything coming together by the end of the story. Normally, we experience something that was mentioned by the end of the book as an 'oh…that fits / I should've seen that'. If you understand the pattern of Tension-Resolution, you can start looking for how something hinted at will come into play later. In the movie *It's a Wonderful Life* there are a number of things involved with Zuzu (the main character's daughter). She wins a flower at school, cares for it by neglecting herself on the walk home, gets the sniffles and a fever, upsets her dad who calls the teacher who he accosts, then winds up at a bar and has the teacher's husband punch him in the mouth...and there's more. At the end of the movie Zuzu hears bells on the Christmas tree and declares that her teacher taught her that when one hears a bell, an angel receives his wings. So, the story resolves nicely since daddy agrees and respects the teacher. If you know to look for patterns then you are in great shape at the end of the story, if you think it through. However, even during the story you could start seeing what is mentioned as a placeholder or hint concerning things to come. Look for patterns, sequences, cause and effect. Teach your children to do the same and they'll be significantly smarter than their peers who haven't put this together.

- Narration is another important practice for growing a great reader. Charlotte Mason, a renowned British educator around 1900, encouraged the practice of reading to students for a few minutes, then having the students retell in their own words what was just read to them (and with any insights that might come to mind). This practice engages more of the senses in actively listening and connecting the patterns. Since books are written to represent spoken language, the reading out loud aspect is quite impactful on appreciating the three-dimensional nature of the written word. In this way, things can 'come alive' for your budding reader.

- SQ3R. This method has been around since the middle of the last century and still holds much to commend it.

Anyone who learns to read effectively by taking in large amounts of information will naturally develop their own version of this method. SQ3R/SQRRR stands for Survey, Question, Read, Recite, and Review. The sequence is important because it follows a solid strategy to cultivate the right mindset for reading anything. It is perfect for essays and articles in the academic world, but still applies to letters and novels and poems. It is important to dispel the false notion that something must be read in the order it is laid out, word by word and sentence by sentence. Of course, your brain can reorganize anything. P-L-U-G can spell GULP, so you probably get the point. Taking in some basic information before you read allows you to look for patterns. Surveying is all about this important ability. In surveying a chapter, we might read a sentence or two at the beginning, read the last paragraph, and look for key phrases in between. Other obvious things are in play like the title and purpose of the chapter. Questions have to do with personal questions you might have about the article or chapter. They relate to what you might learn or think is important. Forming a few questions as a second step sets your mind to look for answers, if not surprises. Reading is the actual reading of the material. Recite, similar to Narration (above), is about expressing briefly in your own words what the section is about, how the patterns fit together. Finally, Review makes sure you've answered your questions and run your mind back over the information one last time. I assure you, though it sounds like work, it is significantly more effective and efficient than re-reading something two or three times. SQ3R is like drawing lines in a parking lot so you can park the cars in a safe and efficient way. Here's a sample worksheet to get you started:

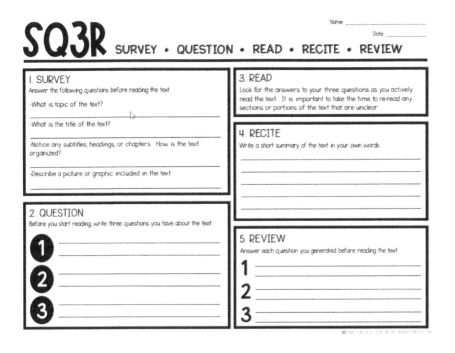

https://litinfocus.com/maximize-reading-comprehension-sq3r/

- Discussion or discussing what you read with another person almost has no peer in the learning process. Even the act of teaching another person (or your stuffed animals) the contents of a chapter or book can have dramatic effects on learning. Organizing information for others requires you to think it through for communication; and frankly, if you make it understandable for someone else, then it's going to be understandable to you. Discussion, however, is a little different. Ideally the other person has read the material too, but it's not necessary. In a discussion. you are weighing the merits, the pros and cons, of the material at hand. When people engage in a dialog about the contents of an article, then they are technically teaching each other. This back-and-forth interaction allows for connections to be made that weren't in play before the discussion. Allowing a child to explain what he has read to you gets it in motion. Adding questions like Who? What? When? Where? Why? How? can create more vigor in the discussions. Personally, we found that having the kids explain and discuss their daily reading with one another was an excellent way to increase comprehension. You can also use our book report format (below) for discussion to multiply learning.

- Book Reports. While technically this should be under the Writing section below, one of the easiest ways to master comprehension is to write a book report, but not the kind you might normally imagine.

The 5 Steps to Great Book Reports

After being challenged on it, I sat down and made up this process for a book report. I wish I had put this together for my kids, but basically, we did something similar as we homeschooled.

1. **Keep the goal in mind:** You want the child intelligently interacting with the book. It really isn't a synopsis, as most book reports seem to be. Instead, it is a summary with some analysis / evaluation.

2. **Try this simple process:**

   FIRST: Have your student make a written list of "6 Things I Liked About the Book" & "6 Things I Did Not Like About the Book." [This is THE MOST IMPORTANT step]

   SECOND: Use this 'form' to sketch out an outline (just use bullet points).

   a. Open your report with "_____ (book title and author) is a _____(summary adjective: good, bad, well-written, fantastic, engaging, awful, etc.) _____ (category: adventure, science fiction, historical novel, etc.) that is about _____ (the very basic overview of the story).

   b. Example: *The Wonderful Wizard of Oz by L. Frank Baum is a delightful children's fantasy novel that is about a girl who makes her way through the strange world of Oz to finally arrive back home in the loving world of her Kansas family and friends.*

c.Give a short (few sentences) summary of the story. This can be done many ways, but the idea is to give someone who hasn't read the book the basics.

d.What I liked about the book and why (2 or 3 is fine).

e.What I didn't like about the book and why (2 or 3 is fine).

f.Conclusion- Usually this will be a recommendation or warning about reading the book.

THIRD: Write it!

FOURTH: Get Help! (somebody reads it and offers corrections / ideas)

FIFTH: Make it GREAT by re-writing the whole thing with the improvements from the 4th Step included.

ADDENDUM: Younger children could go through the steps above as a list to write, or as an oral exercise with mom or dad.

....

I know there are other approaches; use what works as long as it is helping your child really learn to

1. **Think**

2. **Write**

See at: https://advanced-writing-resources.com/how-to-do-book-reports/

Arithmetic

What is arithmetic and what is it for? While there are many reasons to study math, as we've mentioned from time-to-time, learning a language is the chief reason, but measurement is the practical one. Honestly, there are a number of additional side benefits, but the key word in the practical world is 'measurement'. Once we understand the power and influence that comes with accurately measuring things, we have the answer to the age-old question most kids use against the subject, "Why do I need to learn math? I'll never use it!" Measurement is so important we discuss it in a later section for the benefit of how it relates to a healthy homeschool and growing independent learners. For now, just realize that measurement provides for predicting the future. When you travel across country and want to let the in-laws when you'll arrive, *rate x time = distance* (RT=D) can come in pretty handy.

Language is the chief value that arithmetic brings into our lives. However, think about it; if you never live or work or play in a China-oriented world, then knowing Mandarin won't do much for you. Math is the language of science. Math is the water in which all the STEM (Science, Technology, Engineering, and Mathematics) disciplines swim. So, if a child isn't headed to a math-based career, then he may just have a point. And again, if a child does not learn math, then she isn't headed to a math-based career, no matter what. Calculus is the language of physics, so there is no getting around the fact that if one doesn't learn calculus, then they won't be a physicist. There are exceptions in a team context, but at some point, someone better know the math!

What is language? What does it mean that math is a language? Language is basically a systematic way of conveying meaning. By systematic, I mean that it is organized and consistent with various parts 'fitting together' to produce the whole, called language. Math uses symbols and numbers with agreed upon rules to convey meaning unique to mathematics. It isn't complicated except for the fact that it layers information. A symphony piece, like a lengthy math formula, is really not that complicated either. At the basic level a symphony is the layering of percussion (the base) with melody and harmony using strings and wind instruments and chimes, etc. In this sense, music is also a language. Math also breaks down into essentials which are layered into something more complex, if not more beautiful. I only mention this because if we see math as a language, then we can also see that anyone can learn it. All languages are learnable, though there are varying levels of capacity and expertise. Nonetheless, learning the basics and building on them is the key. In part, this is why it is so important to never get behind or skip something in a math curriculum. Indeed, and just like language, math has a use-it-or-lose-it relationship with the learner. Languages are to be used and they can easily slip away over long breaks (like the summer).

There are two other aspects of math that are valuable enough to mention here; logic and absolutes. The nature of math is found in understanding and explaining cause-and-effect. If a = b and b = c, then a = c --- shows the clear nature of If/Then thinking. When one learns the language of math, then she is also learning the nature of logic. In fact, learning formal logic for someone who is skilled at math is often little more than understanding a new vocabulary and a few formulas. Even the way we speak about something not making sense (logic) is found in terms like, "It doesn't add up," or "That does not compute."

Absolutes have fallen on hard times in some quarters because of folks like Nietzsche and the later post-modern influence of everything being relative or in the hands of the one controlling the language. Nonetheless, many things in this world are absolute and either/or in their scope.

Even to say that 'there are no absolutes' is to make a self-defeating declaration. If there are actually no absolutes, then the statement is absolutely true (so then, there's at least one!). Absolutes are always true, which is exactly what math is about apart from mental gymnastics. 1 + 1 = 2 every time, and so the solutions to math problems are always correct or incorrect. It isn't like art or literature where some measure of subjectivity is in play with beauty being in the eye of the beholder.

Engineers do not want to know that the building 'might' withstand hurricane-force winds. They want to know absolutely that the wind and water and steel and concrete have predictable limits. They want to know that it will withstand a Cat-5, and they want to know that absolutely.

Writing

Writing is the top of the pyramid for the '3-Rs', and as such is conquered by the smallest number of people. More of us can read than can effectively use math, and more of us can cipher than can write well. Why might that be? Why is writing harder than reading or learning math? The answer is simply about the number of decisions you must make while doing the activity. Reading has few decisions in it unless you don't know the vocabulary and have to look up words. Arithmetic has very few decisions in it because there are only a few moves in applying a formula or solving for x. When math is hard it is because we are either working on something we do not have the foundation for, or we are simply learning new concepts day-in-and-day-out. If our students did the exact same set of math problems every day, before long they would be caught in utter boredom.

Now, think about writing a paragraph. There are decisions about starting and finishing, about the choice of words, the punctuation, capitalizing certain words, and the various ways we can reorganize what we have written as we write. All this is happening while we are making sure we don't misspell or mistype words as we go along. In any given paragraph you write, there are probably one hundred decisions you could make because of the complexity and diversity of spoken language. No wonder those who can write well seem to have a magic power that others explain by saying, "They just have the gift." There may be a writing gift, just as there may be a walking or talking gift. However, we can all get to a pretty fine level of proficiency if we will but learn. Moreover, given how little competition there is for decent writing, your student can become relatively good even if she is just OK as a writer. Today, most people are not learning how to write at all, so there's just not much competition.

Dr. Jordan Peterson makes the case for how powerful you'll be at the top of any field (yes, in corporations too) by honing your ability to write. He also matches my thoughts about the value of the humanities in our practical world of technology when he says,

> *Over many, many years, you hone your words. They're the most powerful thing about you, bar none. If you are an effective writer and speaker and communicator, you have all the authority and competence that there is. And so, you're at university. Maybe you're taking a humanities degree. Well, what's a humanities degree for? It's to teach you how to think. You learn to think by writing. Now there's more: to read, to speak and all of that, but the best thing you can do is: READ and WRITE every day. Couple of hours every day. Write about things you find important. And see if you can discover what you believe to be true. And that will build you a foundation. And it's unbelievably practical. If you look at people who are phenomenally successful across life, there's various reasons, but one of them is that they're*

unbelievably good at articulating what they're aiming at; and strategizing, and negotiating, and enticing people with a vision forward.

https://www.youtube.com/watch?v=HOXwDWCoqQg

Yes, there is a measure of brainwashing at the university level, but if your child can read and think and write—I promise, they'll have a strong propaganda-immune system!

The power in writing is found in both its ability to communicate and persuade (give a vision forward), and in its ability to cause one to think. This kind of thinking and persuasive ability is at the heart of being an independent learner. The circular benefit of writing has been observed through the ages.

I count myself one of the number of those who write as they learn and learn as they write. -Augustine of Hippo

The Independent Learner Courses

Over the years we discovered that there were ten essential skill we wanted our kids to develop. Though we have discussed them at length, I wanted to include them here. My conviction is that you need to include formal and informal opportunities for your kids to develop these skills. The most efficient way, the easiest way, is to simply get our courses and work through the training with your kids. Nonetheless, approach these skills however you wish, just don't neglect any of them as they contribute with synergy to your student being life-ready. Here is the list with a short explanation of why the skill is valuable.

1.Mastering Reading

In this course we show exactly how to 'hook up' your child's brain to find reading comprehension a natural result of looking at the words. In particular, we give exact exercises to make sense of how words work in relationships, and how the logic of the sentences make sense. To our knowledge, no one has actually developed a process which targets how the brain works with comprehension and logic (this is my favorite course because it really unlocks learning for all).

2.Mastering Writing

There are two courses here. The first is the flagship Writing Course. The second course builds on the writing course by unlocking how to write essays for high school and college. The focus in our training is to teach our students how to understand writing as an intuitive act that makes sense by the sound of the sentences rather than the stilted rules of a grammar book. Rather than trying to teach a series of rote rules, we focus on teaching your student how to think about writing. In fact, all of our courses have the foundation of thinking, which is why our stuff is like nothing else available. Writing daily with our 12 Principles in their toolkit will help your child find her voice and grow her confidence as a writer.

3.Mastering Problem-Solving

Mastering problem-solving is the key to most of what happens in life. It is certainly important in learning mathematics, but there is so much more. Everything one faces in life can be structured as a problem to solve, and mastering this skill is about mastering life. In this extensive course, we introduce an approach that teaches your student to look for a permanent solution rather than a temporary fix. Even employment is about problem-solving; they hire you to solve problems and fire you if you create them!

4.Mastering Focus

Focus is hard to attain because we think 180 degrees wrong about it. As a recovering ADHD-type myself, it took me about 40 years to make sense of what is really happening with focus. We show your student, and you, how to work from the accurate view that lack-of-focus is natural and important. We all are unfocused, but few of us really learn how to 'set up' the game to allow focus to occur instantly and naturally. Here's the way out!

5.Mastering Time

Really, this training is about organizing actions. Most kids (and adults) really don't understand how to organize their actions to get things done. While some of this material is common in the literature, it is honestly uncommon for most folks to have learned these tactics. Here's the place to start organizing actions. If you have a disorganized student, this training will remove his excuses and empower him with a new path.

6.Mastering Goals

There is probably nothing more important than mastering 'how to get what you want' (goals). One student, with challenges learning and functioning, worked through this course and secured a job all by himself as a surprise to his parents (who thought he was unemployable)! Imagine what can happen for your kids.

7.Mastering Memory

The skill of memory can, almost by itself, guarantee success in college and life. If you forget, you lose. Oddly, our brains are magnificently wired to recall massive amount of information once we know exactly how the brain works. I paid for some of college by teaching some of this material. Since then, I've pioneered an approach that considers the uniqueness of the individual in learning to memorize. After this training, your student will be able to memorize a lot of material in a short period of time. What could be more handy?

8.Mastering Communication

Communication is a master skill of success. Lawyers, salespeople, politicians, preachers, teachers, poets, and writers all have shown the amazing effects of using words well. Moreover, family conflict and resolutions are all about learning to be effective with communication. These are the foundational principles that the elite understand, but are also readily available to everyone. We love seeing kids become effective communicators, and you will too.

9.Mastering Relationships

Friendships, dating, marriage...what great difficulties we unnecessarily face by not understanding the basics of what makes relationships (of all kinds) work well. You simply must help your kids learn to relate well with others, which includes the family. Our course will show them (and you) exactly how to make that happen.

10.Mastering Emotions

There is probably no more instantly impactful course than this one for our current age of depression and anxiety. The culture is trying to say there is nothing for your student to do except be offended by others and look for a 'safe place' to hide. Instead, there is another alternative; your student can learn to direct her thinking (and so her emotions). Imagine the gift of giving your child the ability to fix her own upsets and calmly get back into life. This course is the only one we'd say every child on the planet really should complete!

Chapter 12

Key 4: Overcoming Issues

Most of us seem to live in a world of issues without taking actions to make them disappear. With our issues we are not unlike fish; oblivious to what is constantly around them in the way of water. Rather than helping us survive, however, the issues we face commonly suck the life out of us, our families, and our dreams. What issues? Well, consider conflicts in families as a major issue. Also, there are learning challenges, time management, miscommunication, finances, and social isolation or awkwardness. Of course, an issue can be anything that challenges, interferes, or obstructs your path through life. Why do we have these things? While it isn't the question I think you should be asking, it is akin to a long-term conversation about something called Theodicy (Why does a benevolent God allow evil in this world?) or the Problem of Pain, as C.S. Lewis addressed it. In the Christian faith there are two basic lines of thought that roughly match most other religions and philosophies. Instead of evil or pain, it seems the more practical word for all of us is suffering. Why is there suffering?

1. One answer is concerned with the definition of suffering (and evil / pain). In this view, the problem of suffering has to do with the corruption of something good or ideal. They call this a 'privation' or 'lack / absence of good'; championed by Augustine. In this view, suffering is related to a perception of

evil, but not evil as a real 'entity' in this world. Moth holes in a sweater are considered 'evil' because we don't think sweaters should have moth holes.

2. The other answer looks at suffering as a means of guiding (or driving) us to grow and mature as individuals. In this view, we start out separated from God/good and are in the process of bridging that gap with our own growth as we encounter the challenges of the way the world (nature) works. Irenaeus championed this view.

Why am I bringing up philosophy/theology? The answer is that if you don't know how to think about challenges and suffering, you'll simply multiply the problems in your life. The question I think we should ask is, "What do we do about these issues?"

In my thinking and experience, I've concluded that a blend of these views is the way to go. Teaching our kids how to think about suffering and how to benefit from it is a reasonable path that adds the kind of people the world needs at every moment. When you get down to it, the keys are Perception & Virtue.

Perception

Perception is simply the conclusion you make about what you're viewing. Humans are quick to make a story about what they see in order to take the right kind of action. I heard a nice example of the way we interpret things some years ago involving rain. Imagine it's bedtime on a Sunday night and a strong rain comes along outside while you are warmly drifting off to sleep. How does that feel to you? Now, imagine a farmer and his wife who are about to give up their homestead because of a severe drought. Suddenly, the rain comes that will save the farm! How do you imagine they feel? Finally, a young bride has an outdoor wedding and is walking down the aisle when the same strong rain starts pouring on the event. How do you think she feels about the rain?

It's simply raining, but depending on what each person believes it means, they experience varying degrees of joy or misery. It is a matter of interpretation, a matter of the story we tell ourselves, a matter of perception. When issues and suffering come along, the way we interpret what's happening can make all the difference in the world. In particular, we need to answer a specific question, "Is this thing that is happening personal or is it predictable?" Almost always you will find that the universe is not out to get you, as the Bible says, "For he makes His sun rise on the evil and on the good, and sends rain on the just and on the unjust." (Matthew 5:45, ESV). We interpret bad things happening because of our perspective, but most things are neither bad nor good in-and-of-themselves.

In your homeschool, you might have both learning challenges and easy students. Your teen kids might be popular or nerdy. You might have some who love reading and others who love working with their hands. These are just the challenges that come with life. We have a child with cerebral palsy, one who turned out having epilepsy, and one who is almost flawless at math. So what? They all grew up to deal with their challenges and gifts, somewhat in spite of our parenting successes and missteps. What we wanted to do more than anything was to help them understand the things that happen as important parts of the story that would become their lives.

When Tripp was a youngster with CP, we kept stressing to him that having one side of his body that didn't work right was simply a way God would guide him into what he would do in life. Instead of thinking about limitations, we focused him on asking, "What CAN I do?" One day he came in with a pair of inline-skates and dropped them on the floor to proclaim, "Well, that's one thing I can't do!" He went on to learn to snow ski, graduate from the University of Texas with honors, achieve a Masters in Fine Arts, write novels, and so much more. At sixteen years old he gave a message to a group of pastors in Mbali, Uganda. "When I am weak, then I am strong," he told them, quoting the Apostle Paul. These pastors, loaded with hardships, suddenly realize that America had no magic for giving anyone a perfect life. Instead, they learned that things simply happen. It's not personal, it just is. What we do with these challenges is a matter of virtue.

Virtue

Imagine for yourself a character, a model personality, whose example you determine to follow, in private as well as in public.
-Epictetus

Be imitators of me, as I am of Christ. -The Apostle Paul

Virtue is about doing the good or the right thing you understand, without regard to the opinions of others. In this sense it is a lone walk in the right direction. In this sense, it is not for those who are essentially satisfied with their current character or skill-set. The pursuit of virtue is the pursuit of something better. And yet, the moment you imagine yourself better, you have admitted you are not in the place you wish to be as a person.

There is nothing that matches our efforts in preparing our children for life like virtue. The important question to ask must be, "Is my child's virtue a fixed thing?" If you conclude that your child is genetically (or other) fixed in their path, then this idea will be wasted on you and you might as well skip ahead a bit. On the other hand, if you believe a child can be encouraged to choose a virtuous path, then you are a candidate for this important solution to life. History, the Bible, and common sense all agree that virtue is a noble (and possible) path for our lives; yet, so few seem to believe such a thing in our confused day. For example, on one extreme some describe sexual orientation as a matter of genetic destiny, while on the other extreme it's a matter of personal declaration. Virtue wouldn't necessarily address such a thing on that level, but rather would consider the question from the vantage point of what a morally excellent life would be for the individual. Everyone in our family came to the conclusion that a sexually pure life is reserved for marriage; which is the very thing we all pursue before, during, and after the pledge of a life together. All five kids are now married, and would affirm this value to this day. Virtues are not limited to volatile areas only, but include the classical virtues of prudence, justice, temperance, and courage. Christianity added the virtues of faith, hope, and love to the Greek ideals. While the pursuit of virtue is an individual matter, the rejection or neglect of all virtues has widespread impact. A virtueless world is a possibility, but a virtueless home is a tragedy.

How will this help us grow?

If it isn't obvious yet, you will grow as you learn important skills and pursue a virtuous life. Growth, however, is attached to a 'dirty' word in our culture: CHANGE. All growth involves change, so you might as well get used to it. Working on the issues we face means that we are discarding the things that are hindering us from progress; it means we are changing. The change is from bad to good, and then from good to better. Growth is the thing to embrace for yourself, your kids, and your marriage/parenting relationship. In schooling, we refer to growth as learning, and that works too.

Your Issues (Personal)

Unless you are deceived or are reading this in heaven, you probably have noticed that you aren't perfect, that you have a few issues. In this section, I want to address how to think about what you are facing. Why? Well, it is likely your own personal issues interfere with both you and your homeschool experiencing the level of success you want. True? We are going to look at a number of questions here in order to see what practical steps we can apply. There's an old saying from the eastern and addiction traditions that is helpful to bear in mind:

You are enslaved by what you deny.

That's on target. Until you can put your eyes in your head and see the issues you face, then there is no path available except one of servitude to the problem. One simple hint, when you can't see the issue, surrounds the excuses you create. The more we excuse ourselves and our behavior, the more chained we become to the problem. Finally, in my years of counseling, coaching, and training others, I have come to one simple conclusion about emotional, mental, and physical health as human beings:

The more truth you tell, the healthier you become.

There are probably some offline exceptions, but as a confident rule, truth heals. How do you get to the truth? Jesus and Socrates both used the surprisingly powerful tool of questions. Yes, questions are a simple and effective way to seek out the truth. Let's get going.

What are my issues?

Asking yourself to identify your own issues is an excellent-and-humble way to begin, since it assumes you have issues. You do have issues, everyone does. First, however, we probably need to define what we mean here. An issue is essentially something that is interfering with or hindering your progress in life. If you have no interest in making progress, then you probably don't have an issue at all. On one level you might think of this as skills or habits you need. If you lived in a world like a fishing village on an island in Polynesia in the 1400s, then not being able to read would not be much of an issue for your life and livelihood. But in our industrialized, modern world, it is essential that one reads. If reading is important to your career and you are a poor reader, then learning to read better is an issue for you.

It is more common to think of issues as those belonging to psychology or character. Being explosively angry, or having crippling anxiety or depression, can easily interfere with your progress in life. Until you identify an issue and accept it, all you will be filled with are excuses and denial. The solution itself will come from clarity about your issue. If you are depressed because you lost a loved one, then medication is less likely to be a solution. It's processing the loss and re-focusing on life that will lift the despair. If things are going just right in your life and you are depressed, then medication may be a good fit.

Homeschooling itself is loaded with common issues; time-management, discipline, keeping up with assignments, conflict, and paper-work to name a few. Never mind all the things that go into the operation of a home. If any of these hinder your homeschooling efforts, then you may safely assume you have an issue to overcome. Not being in a public school can also diminish other problems (like the 'attitude' commonly brought home by those fledglings in middle school). Your issues will be related to what you want. So, try this simply approach:

1. List everything you want for your kids and homeschool. Just make a massive list over a few days. You can

always delete things later on. If you think you might want it, then write it down.

2. List all the actions that need to happen for each want you have.

3. Ask, "Why is this action not happening? Why else? Why else?

These questions, when answered, will show you the issues you need to overcome to get what you want.

An example may help here. Let's assume you want your teenagers to be self-sufficient by the time they leave home. Actions that might go into becoming self-sufficient would include things like doing their own laundry, making their bed, maintaining their own bank account, shopping for their own clothes, and getting themselves to complete their schoolwork without your nagging or presence. Now, when you look at actions, then you can learn a lot. Why is my teenager not doing her own laundry? Perhaps you do the laundry for everyone. Perhaps they don't know how, or perhaps you've never required it. Self-sufficiency is the issue here, but it shows up in much smaller ways, which also means that it can be cured in much smaller ways. Now go work on these three questions and see what gets uncovered.

More Tricks from the Goody Bag

There are a few additional strategies that can help you sort out your issues, as we will share in a moment. Please bear in mind that my understanding is that most issues are about us not telling ourselves the truth about something. Additionally, this kind of 'lying' is commonly hidden from us on any kind of conscious level. The key is to get it out into the open, out into your own thoughtful-and-conscious processing. The following are a few strategies you might find incredibly helpful.

Keep asking, "Why?"

Toyota likes to use 'Why?" up to five times in a row. JT Foxx (an entrepreneur coach) likes six 'Whys?" in a row. Personally, I think you simply need to use as many as it takes. The purpose of asking 'Why?' is to get underneath whatever is on the surface of an issue. Similar to breaking up, quitting a job, or leaving a church; the reason isn't THE reason. People don't share the real reason at first; perhaps because they are shy or fearful, or perhaps because they simple aren't aware of the real reason themselves. Basically, all you are doing is continuing to ask the 'Why?" question until you get to something insightful or important. Take procrastination as an example.

I procrastinate on doing my taxes.

Why?

I don't know where everything is?

Why?

It's scattered in a bunch of different files.

Why?

I don't know how to organize it all?

Why?

I'm more creative, but more scattered in my thoughts.

Why?

I never learned how to focus or organize things.

Why?

Mother was sick most of my childhood.

Why?

She had Grambel-Kniffen's Syndrome (not a real thing).

Why?

Genetics.

So, why haven't you learned to focus and organize things?

I never had it explained & I never practiced it.

So, there you have it. You might need to go back a few 'Whys' in order to focus on the issue, but underneath it all you can see that this person simply never had it modeled or explained or practiced. The relief and insight mean that they can get in motion; go find out how to organize it from a friend, mentor, YouTube, Udemy course, or trial-and-error approach. Next, practice until you own it.

Ask, "How will life be different?"

The power in this question is in its invitation to look ahead to a better future. Our imaginings about the future are very powerful. If we imagine the future will be worse because of a particular action, we will invariably act in ways to avoid that future. On the other hand, if we imagine how the future will be better, then we'll tend to take actions in that direction. One of the easier ways to think about your future is to consider how life will be different if you _____ (fill in some result or outcome here). For example, if you think about becoming a person who is always optimistic about whatever is going on, how will things be different? You can imagine that people will probably enjoy being around you, and then you will be the one who gets everyone to start thinking of positive ways to solve the problem at hand. You also could imagine that you don't hide in your room under the covers as often, or that you go ahead and take quick actions to produce results. All of this thinking is coming about because you are imagining yourself becoming a more positive person. Realizing these benefits in your imagination can become a great impetus to change.

Ponder, "Why work on my weakness?"

Most of my adult life I have emphasized the notion that we should be finding our gifting, our talents, our strengths, and serving others with them. Our weaknesses should be 'buttressed', so they don't create problems in our life. While that makes sense and is certainly true, it isn't all that's true. If you can think about what is holding you back (known as 'constraints theory' in some circles), then you can realize that overcoming the very thing that is hindering you is among the most powerful efforts that can make a great difference. Christian Swartz illustrates this idea with a barrel having a stave broken off:

The idea is that the barrel can only fill up to the level of the lowest stave or slat. Obviously, if you want more water in the barrel, then the stave must be raised. This is a simple way to understand limits or constraints. What in your life is limiting you? Of course, it's probably your point of weakness. While it can make sense to improve your strengths, it's probably even more powerful to turn your weakness into a strength. Is that possible? Well, if you can't read can you learn to read well? If you can't speak publicly, can you learn to be a really good speaker? Of course you can! Some things may be impossible (I'm 5'6" tall and in my 60's… I'm not going to dunk a basket); so, don't work on those. Imagine what a good plan and a lot of practice might do for you if you removed the very thing holding you, or your homeschool back! Yes, strengths are very important, but weaknesses hold us back. Think of it this way, "Maximize your strengths. But optimize your weaknesses."

What if trying doesn't count?

"At least I tried," or "I tried my best." These kinds of phrases are almost a given, a cliché, or a mantra in our society. If we reason a bit, isn't it pretty easy to see why this way of thinking really doesn't help you solve much of anything? It really is a matter of how one defines success or winning. In most dictionaries, success is defined as reaching the desired outcome. That makes sense, doesn't it? If your team wins the Super Bowl, then they succeeded. If they lost, but you proclaim, "Well, they tried their best," what are you actually communicating? Is the aim to try hard and hope luck turns things in the direction you want? Is trying hard really a success when you actually fail? There are two points I want to invite you to ponder in this regard:

A. It could just be an excuse.

B. Imagine your life if trying doesn't count.

I'm not politically correct here at all, but if you are open to the truth, then you'll see that this notion of 'trying hard' or 'trying your best' is simply a readymade excuse. It is common for us to excuse our behavior, but it is a nasty habit that really doesn't serve us well at all. It is a kind of comfort to our feelings, or to those of our kids. And yet, is it comforting? What are we actually trying to say? You tried hard, but winning or succeeding doesn't really matter at all, so good job? If you are educating your child at home, does trying to read really cut it? Does trying to brush their teeth count? No, indeed! You actually want an outcome; that is the focus of the effort and the standard of success. Success and failure are about getting it to happen (whatever 'it' is). My kids could never have played in the NBA (genetics & interest are the issues), so why would I commend them for pursuing a career in something they are guaranteed to fail in? I don't want to misdirect them or comfort them. Really, I just want them to succeed because they pursued something that made sense and they worked hard to make it happen.

Of course, this leads to the second point of wondering what life might be like if trying didn't count. Excuses would disappear and focus would burst on the scenes; at least, that's my best guess. Go back to the 'learning to read' example. If the point is not that we are going to try to learn to read, but rather that we are going to learn to read...how will that affect an approach to homeschool? I'm guessing it'll be pretty dramatic. If you are going to educate your children and grow them into independent learners who can teach themselves, then that homeschool will look DRAMATICALLY DIFFERENT than a homeschool that is going to 'try' to educate their kids.

Thinking we are going to 'try' to learn math facts is quite different than thinking we ARE going to learn our math facts. Stripping the excuse away is a great way for you to overcome your own issues. If you have an anger problem, then 'trying to do better' is a terrible approach compared to saying, "I will not simply try, but I will figure out how to reign in my anger and remain calm." Stop trying. Figure it out. Win. Yoda was probably right when he said, "There is no try..." Quit conjuring up excuses, my young padawan. Instead, figure it out, work hard, succeed and win.

How do you change a belief?

Some years ago, I called my friend, Dr. Keith Bower. He was published in college (Chemistry), studied theology and received a master's degree, studied philosophy and received a master's degree, then went on to get his PhD (which explored something about mathematics and theology). So, I thought he might know about changing beliefs.

"Hey Keith, Fred."

"Hey Fred, how's it going?"

"Good…I've got a philosophical question for you."

"Shoot."

"How do we come to believe something?"

Long Pause…

Second Long Pause…

Keith chuckles…

"That, my friend, is something no one seems to have figured out."

Whew, so it wasn't just me! How we come to believe something to be true is a bit tricky. The proof is kind of obvious, since no matter what the media, professors, preachers, salespersons, or moms try, we don't all, always, buy it. But beliefs do really rule at the center of most of our issues in life, since they are part of the Story/Fiction in The Great Pyramid.

One glaring example to me has been the number of women who have shared in counseling their difficulty with thinking of God as their father, when their father had been abusive or untrustworthy. That makes some sense, doesn't it? You grow up as a little girl and come to some definite conclusions about your daddy. It would be reasonable to suspect any other 'fathers' to be met with suspicion, even evoking difficult emotions to process.

While that is dramatic, and understandable, most of us deal with our beliefs on a more subtle level. We all have beliefs (just think of the word 'conclusion' and you'll get it) about so many things that affect us daily; public speaking, how we look, how we manage our time, what love means, and how our spouses should act in public. In some ways, it makes us all crazy, since our different beliefs tend to generate different actions. Of course, it gets even messier because we look at others' actions and make a guess (often wrong) about what belief is behind what they're doing. What a mess.

Interestingly enough, while I don't know exactly how to create a belief, I do know how to kill one...no, really, I do. Think about it for a moment. A belief is a conclusion you have come to about something. It may be as simple as 'bad kids prove the parents are bad too' (nope!), or 'all white/black/brown/green people are racists'. It also just could be that you believe if you read the Bible every day, you won't get sick.

Honestly, there are likely thousands-upon-thousands of beliefs you have. So what? Well, when they become OBSTRUCTIVE BELIEFS it can be a problem. These kinds of beliefs will hinder our actions and reactions in life. If a belief isn't a problem, it isn't a problem. On the other hand...

So, what's up with these conclusions or beliefs we have about the way things should go in certain situations. Actually, it is simple: A belief is an unchallenged conclusion that there is one-and-only-one possibility concerning what you are looking at. If someone looks at you with a frown and you conclude that they are mad at you, then that is what you 100% believe if there are no other possibilities in front of you. If you actually think that you don't know why they frowned, then you will simply not have a belief (maybe we should call it a 'conviction', too).

So, that's it. As soon as you know there are two or three possibilities that could also possibly be true, you will no longer 'believe'— whatever it is. Yes, they did frown. Maybe they are mad at you. Maybe they have a stomach bug. Or, maybe they are upset because they just found out their dad has stage four colon cancer. There's a saying that gets to the point:

You Can Doubt Anything If You Question It Enough

Pretty much, that's how it goes. Unfortunately, it takes both motivation and objectivity, of which humans often have in very short supply. Nonetheless, if you want a belief to die—just come up with a few other reasonable (not better) possibilities. While you are always in search of the truth, knowing there are other explanations for what you see can dramatically free you to see the truth you seek.

Bear in mind that if you are able to remove some of your hurtful beliefs about homeschooling (I must teach my kids or they won't learn * My kids must be happy now to be happy adults * I can't homeschool if my spouse doesn't help * Kids who aren't motivated have learning disabilities * I have to change things if they don't like school * What's important is that they think I'm the greatest mom ever, etc.). Here's a process I've developed that may help you. It is certainly better with a coach I've trained, but if you play with it a bit, I bet you can see dramatic results as you uncover, and kill, OBSTRUCTIVE BELIEFS.

This process needs practice. If you want a personal session, we can possibly arrange that (I'm crazy good at this, if I have room in my schedule) if you will contact me via the information in the back of this book. Nonetheless, if you'll try it with ten obstructive beliefs, I bet you'll see plenty of benefit in your life.

FINDING AN OBSTRUCTIVE BELIEF [© Dr. Fred Ray Lybrand Jr, 2019]

1. WHAT DO YOU WANT? I want to…

2. WHAT WILL IT TAKE? It will take…

3. WILL IT WORK? Yes / No

4. (IF NO) WHAT WILL WORK? What will work is…

5. WHY AREN'T YOU DOING IT? I'm not doing it because…

6. DO YOU BELIEVE THAT? YES / NO (If 'No' start over)

    a. START HERE (STATE THE BELIEF): I believe that…

    b. ASSUME A CLUSTER OF BELIEFS ARE INVOLVED (you may want to discover them in the due course of time).

ELIMINATING OBSTRUCTIVE BELIEFS [© Dr. Fred Ray Lybrand Jr, 2019]

1. WHAT'S THE OBSTRUCTIVE BELIEF THAT FEELS TRUE (OR SORT OF TRUE) TO YOU? I believe that

_____.

2. HOW SURE DO YOU FEEL THAT IT'S TRUE? ___%

3. HOW WOULD THINGS BE DIFFERENT IF IT WASN'T TRUE? WHY? (3X)

    a. If it wasn't true, things would be different...

        i. Because...

    b. If it wasn't true, things would be different...

        i. Because...

    c. If it wasn't true, things would be different...

        i. Because...

4. WHAT COULD ALSO POSSIBLY BE TRUE (EVEN THE OPPOSITE)? WHY? (3X)

    a. It could also be true that...

        i. Because...

    b. It could also be true that...

        i. Because...

    c. It could also be true that...

        i. Because...

5. SO NOW, HOW SURE ARE YOU THAT IT'S TRUE? ___%

*REPEAT TILL GONE

6. STRATEGY

a. One thing I can do is…

b. One thing I can do is…

c. One thing I can do is…

So, there's the form. Please play with it a dozen times before you 'conclude' it doesn't work for you!

[A final note here concerns one's belief in God as an example. I am convinced that God's existence is the undeniable conclusion of a rational-and-honest thought process. However, if you question it enough, you might be able to conclude God is dead or doesn't exist. Just having questions won't kill a belief unless the options are actually plausible. So, can nothing create something? I don't see how, hence God. Can unintelligence create intelligence, I don't see how. Can an unconscious (not self-aware) universe, create a conscious (self-aware) universe? I don't see how). So, for me, questioning God's existence actually makes me surer He is there. Questioning truth will prove truth, while questioning falsehood (most of your OBSTRUCTIVE BELIEFS) will cause them to crumble before you.]

Enjoy.

What's the biggest secret for change?

If you didn't really grasp the full explanation above, let me leave you with a simpler way to understand change. The decades of counseling others that I experienced showed me a basic fact: The closer to the truth, the healthier the person. Schizophrenia is basically a break with reality, so these sufferers are the extreme example of those who are the farthest from the truth. When addicts are in 'denial' about their enslavement, they are in the midst of being unhealthy. As we learn to stare at the truth of things and not blink, we take a step forward. Even on the practical level of finances, when we don't know the truth of what we are spending or have in our account, our 'financial health' suffers. If you want your kids to be healthier, then invite them to see the truth. Quit over-protecting them. Stop sugar-coating everything. Don't tell them they are Einstein or Picasso when they are growing up. Everyone is better off with a growth mindset, which is what learning is all about. You learn more truth as you grow (stoves can burn you), and you benefit in powerful ways (stay clear of hot stoves). If you want to see change, stick to figuring out the truth. In our wild postmodern world where truth is largely what you want it to be, you won't be as popular. However, you will grow kids who will eventually appreciate you for what you gave them. I think that's the truth.

THEIR ISSUES (CHILDREN)

Children have issues too. In fact, the issues children have are usually the same one's adults have, so there issues are kind of your issues. With kids, however, we have a great deal of influence, though nothing is guaranteed. Your calling is to give them the life skills and perspective to do well in this world, and in the next one too.

WHAT ARE THEIR ISSUES? Children can have all kinds of issues, including learning challenges, behavioral challenges, and emotional challenges. In large measure, challenges are often associated with weaknesses, as we discussed earlier. The most important thing here is that issues are challenges; therefore, they are all things to overcome. Does your child have dyslexia? So what? Get help, work at it, figure it out. Empower your child to overcome their challenges in line with what your hopes, and their hopes, suggest. We've already walked you through our experience with Tripp, our oldest who has cerebral palsy. There were plenty of other challenges; some were less organized, others were more upsetting, while others were a little too obsessive. As your kids age, the issues will involve relationships and faith and independence. The most significant thing I can share is the lesson one of my mentors, Dr. Marlon Howe, taught me concerning teenage rebellion. Basically, he offered that rebellious teens are trying to 'get in' or they are trying to 'get out'. Perhaps there is more to it than that, but I've observed it to be a pretty consistent pattern. If your child doesn't feel included or a part of the family, then rebellious actions are often a cry to get attention in order to belong. If your child feels trapped and oppressed and controlled, then it is likely that rebellion is generated by a desire to escape and become their own person.

We found that avoiding having 'favorite' children helped the most. I would explain to the kids that I loved them all equally, but that I loved their mother more. In this way we emphasized that the core of the family was our marriage relationship. Knowing that tends to free up a child to not feel they must be there emotionally to take care of mom or dad. It also had the added benefit of building into their thinking the idea that they didn't have to always stick around, but that they are commissioned to go find their own mate and build their own life, if that's what they wanted.

There are other things that help kids feel included, such as receiving fair treatment, having their own personal things and spaces, while also being in on family events and outings. The simplest thing we ever did that seemed to make a big difference was to hug the kids in groups of two, three, and more. Yes, we should hug our kids, but too much of individual hugging can miscommunicate. "Mommy hugs her longer / more often," can get stuck in the head of a child. Just hug them in groups as well as individually; it's hard to conclude there's a favorite that way. Having a favorite child is a shortcut to inciting jealousy, conflict, and rebellion. If you can't help it, then go to your pastor or a counselor and get some help.

WHY ARE THERE ISSUES? You probably already know the answer to this one, but let's underscore the answer; children are to be nurtured and taught to become happy adults. That's really all there is to it. Of course, family dysfunction and personality and traumas can all contribute to issues. However, humans are not 'mostly instinct' like animals. Humans go from not knowing how to knowing how. Issues for kids are all about that movement, maturing into solid independent individuals. Your independent learner doesn't start out knowing how to read, but they need to learn how to read. All of the things in the way are issues (or obstacles) that you can help remove in the course of time. Broadening tastes, learning vocabulary, staying focused, and reviewing content all add up to getting a life-skill that will help them in limitless ways throughout their lives. Now, simply substitute anything that needs to be learned for 'knowing how to read' and you'll be on your way. Knowing how to share, how to calm themselves, how to do things they don't feel like doing, etc., all add up to overcoming issues.

WHAT DO I DO? You simply want to help them learn how to teach themselves how to overcome their own challenges as they mature and develop the skills they need for a successful life. Frankly, just go back to the previous material on how to overcome your own issues. All of those things apply to kids just as well. Teach them about working on weaknesses, as well as developing strengths. Help them learn how to overcome obstructive beliefs; use the same form with them. Make use of The 4 Magic Questions to build the behaviors and habits your child needs for life (see the next section for this powerful tool). Finally, keep a diet of healthy books on their list. Reading excellent biographies, and history, and virtuous literature can help shape a child dramatically. If it fits your world, have them read the Bible, the writings of Epictetus, and The Book of Virtues; age-appropriate, of course. We found the books in the Robinson Curriculum matched this goal of reading wholesome literature, but find your own way. Indeed, you might want to read a few of them for yourself!

HOW WILL LIFE BE DIFFERENT? There is no way to know how life would have been with some other path, but we can make an educated guess. If you overcome your issues and help your child mature into a happy adult, how would you bet? Imagine loading them with the skills of reading, writing, math, memory, emotional maturity, problem-solving, spirituality, discipline, and effective 'goal-setting'. How will that person contribute to your home? How will that person contribute to the world? Imagine developing a virtuous person who takes on their own responsibility for continued growth in life. How will that individual pursue purpose in this world, in their brief life? Basically, it falls back to a couple of proverbs that direct us as parents on a path of wisdom:

The rod and reproof give wisdom, but a child left to himself brings shame to his mother. -Proverbs 29:15

Train up a child in the way he should go; even when he is old he will not depart from it. -Proverbs 22:6

I'm not directing you about techniques (like spanking), but rather about principles. There are more specifics I'll share later in the book under <u>The 7 Outcomes of Your Successful Homeschool,</u> but the basic idea is right here. When children are left without guidance and direction, they'll tend to turn out poorly. When children are trained, they tend to keep a lot of the good stuff. The future ahead can be bright for your child, even in a world that seems dark at times. You are in a great, but temporary, position of influence. You have what you need to do well contained in the thoughts I've shared in this book. And yet, there is oh so much you can learn and teach me. It is in this sense that we are helping to point one another in the right directions. Bless you in your labors for your family.

Chapter 13

Key 5: Permanent Problem-Solving

Problem-solving is one of the ultimate skills for both homeschooling the independent learner and for life in general. In fact, it is the reason people are hired to do a job. When your child is hired someday, it will be for the purpose of solving some kind of problem for their employer. From engineering to customer service to management, there is a problem that an employee is there to solve. Even superficially this is important to know because of the three ways a job can go:

- If you solve the problem you're hired to solve, then you'll keep your job.

- If you solve more problems than you're hired to solve, you'll get a raise/promotion.

- If you create more problems than you solve, you'll be fired.

Even more important is understanding that problem-solving is a life-skill that will serve you and your students until death. Imagine if you get really good at solving problems? Health, relationships, money, crises, and everything else in life involves problem-solving at some level or another. A few years ago, I developed carpal-tunnel in both hands. It was a little weird and a little scary, especially since I type a lot. Using what I'm going to share here, I saw my problem go away within a couple of months; never to return (that was three years ago). What things do you, your students, or your homeschool face that would make a difference if they went away forever? Finally, problem-solving is the skill your students should apply to math. Yes, math is the training for problem-solving. Kids who don't do okay in math commonly don't learn the critical skills of analysis, logic, or endurance. Let's dig in.

Problem-Soothing: The Wrong Way to Do It

Have you ever noticed how you can gain weight, lose weight, and then gain it back? How about conflict in your life? Doesn't it seem to get resolved, go away, but then come back again? The reason is that you are engaged in a problem-solving pattern that oscillates. Commonly, we call it something like "treating the symptoms." The reason for this problem-soothing approach is related to the pain we experience. The cycle is easy to understand, and all credit is due to Robert Fritz in pointing this one out to me. It works as follows:

1. Something causes 'pain' (the problem)

2. You take action

3. The pain lessens

4. The action lessens

5. The problem continues

Kind of simple, isn't it? You're overweight…you diet…you lose weight…you stop the diet…the overweight returns. You have a conflict…you talk…things feel better…you quit talking…conflict returns. This kind of back-and-forth game can go away if you can really deal with the problem with a permanent solution mindset. What would you like to weigh for the rest of your life? How can this conflict issue go away forever between us? Even asking those questions can set you on a better path. Technically, you are moving from problem-soothing, to creating the result you really want. Creating a solution that lasts is far superior to any kind of temporary problem-soothing effort. My advice is to stop it! Just give up on short-term, symptom-treating, problem-soothing strategies. They waste time because they won't work over the long haul. Work on lasting solutions, on permanent problem-solving, on creating the results you want to see.

The Permanent Mindset

The secret problem-solving mindset is to think about forever. Yes, think about how a problem can be solved in such a way it is never a problem again. Of course, I'm not talking about basic math problems or where you left your keys, right? Well, math yes, your keys, no. If you misplace your keys on a regular basis, you are likely engaged in problem-soothing. If you counted up the minutes-to-hours you spent looking for your keys, you might find it's a bigger problem than you think. What if you ask a simple question like, "How can I never have a problem with misplacing my keys ever again?" Most likely it will lead to a lasting solution. A mom might answer, "I have a place for my keys; my purse. My purse also always has a place it stays. The kids know to move my purse to its 'place' if they find it somewhere else. They also know to put my keys in my purse if they find them." Even better, use the principle of redundancy. Have two places your purse can stay (different ends of the house). Have two places your keys can stay (in your purse or on in the corner of the kitchen counter). If you settle into this approach, your keys can always be found quickly, period. If you think this is too simple to be an example, then you still don't see the power of principles. Complex manufacturing, programming, and communication all work the same way when you think about solving a problem permanently. Warning: Many problems can't be solved permanently; however, this is clearly the way to think about it. Even if you can't find a permanent solution, the quality of the solutions you do find will greatly improve. At the very least, they won't be any worse than the problem-soothing ideas you'll come up with otherwise.

The 9 Parts of Permanent Problem-Solving

"If I had an hour to solve a problem, I'd spend 55 minutes thinking about the problem and five minutes thinking about solutions." -Albert Einstein

The following information is a summary of my Permanent Problem-Solving Model and is found in our course on Problem-Solving at www.independenthomeschool.com. The list is sequential, but it's a form not a formula. Think about Jazz. There isn't a formula for the music, but there is a basic form it follows. If you'd like to understand this idea, listen to an old video of Bing Crosby and Louie Armstrong performing 'That's Jazz' from High Society, 1956. Frankly, the order of the permanent problem-solving form is pretty important, so don't skip around until you own the skill for yourself. It takes practice, but once you master the basics your life will change for the better. These nine parts are posed as questions, which is our best tool for learning.

1. What is the real problem?

Most people who have spent any time professionally solving problems know that how you define the problem dictates the kinds of solutions you'll consider. Imagine your child struggling with math. If you define the problem as a 'my child doesn't have a math chip', then there isn't much in the way of solutions to consider. If you define the problem as 'my child doesn't have the basics down', then the solution will have something to do with working on the basics. If you define the problem as 'the math curriculum is no good', then the solution will involve finding a better curriculum. See how that works? If you mis-define the problem, you'll need to be outrageously lucky to get even close to the solution you really need. Defining the problem isn't as hard as you might think, provided you embrace a couple of important distinctions.

a. Problem vs. Reality

There is no bigger waste of time than attempting to solve a problem that doesn't exist. One day our first child bit into an apple and suddenly let out an 'ow' that startled me. He said, "My tooth!" I instantly started to 'solve the problem' by getting on to him to be more careful about biting an apple. The problem was that there wasn't a problem. He was about five years old and it was his first baby tooth to lose! Baby teeth fall out, that's reality. If you have a reality and call it a problem, then you are going to be swimming in the deep water of unsolvable frustration. Theologically speaking, pretend for a moment there actually is a permanent 'hell', and you wind up in it. You wouldn't have a problem; you'd have a reality. You are not getting out, so there is nothing to solve. Figuring out how to deal with a reality is quite different from solving a problem. The first thing you want to do is to separate the thing you are facing by dividing the parts that are realities from the parts that are not. Realities can't be changed. Yes, sometimes you don't know if a change is possible, so leave it in the potential problem pile. Especially look at time. If there is not enough time for a particular solution, then the reality is that there isn't time for that particular solution. Keep the things that are unchangeable parts of reality separate from the rest. You can't solve a reality.

b. Problems don't exist until...

The truth is that are no problems on the planet. In fact, there are no problems anywhere at all. You can't even name something that is a problem. A

Supreme Court decision? Not a problem? A hurricane? No problem there. A lying witness that lets a criminal off scot free? Not even close to a problem. These aren't problems by their existence, rather they become problems the moment something happens. Problems don't exist until somebody wants something. That's what actually makes a 'thing' a 'problem'. If you want the Supreme Court decision to be the opposite of what they decided, you have a problem. If you want the hurricane to drift out to sea and it does, you have no problem. If you are the criminal and get off scot-free, you have no problem. Understanding this aspect of defining a problem can move your solution-creating skill to a professional level. How much better for homeschooling? Keep asking, "What do I want?" Keep asking, "What do they want?" These questions will usually guide you to a far more strategic definition of a problem to solve. In homeschooling, you might consider it a problem that teaching your children takes so much of your time. If I were sitting in your kitchen chatting about this over a cup of coffee, the conversation would probably change.

You: Ugh, it takes so much time to prepare and teach the kids.

Me: Why is that a problem?

You: Because I don't know these subjects and I haven't read the books, so I have to spend a lot of time getting ready to teach the lessons.

Me: Why do you think you have to do school along with your kids?

You: Because that's how it works. You have to know it to teach it.

Me: OK, so what do you want?

You: I want to have more time to prepare.

Me: Let me try again. What do you want for your kids regarding homeschool?

You: I want them to learn what they need to learn and develop the character they need for life.

Me: So, their learning is the real problem. Right?

You: Yes.

Me: So, if they learn, then the problem is solved?

You: Yes.

Me: So, the problem is all about how to get them to learn.

You: Right.

Me: There's another part of what you want isn't there? Don't you want homeschool not take up so much of your time?

You: Yes!

Me: So, the problem is found in asking, "How can I help my kids learn without it taking up so much of my time?"

You: Yes, that makes sense.

Me: So, that's the direction you want to go. Ask yourself, "How can I permanently help my kids learn without it taking up so much of my time?"

Now, if we skip ahead, one of the solutions could be the one we found for our homeschool; turn the students into the teachers. If the children become their own teachers, then your role becomes one of making sure that they are actually learning. The issue then becomes about how you measure their progress. What's funny is that they already are their own teachers, especially when we well-meaning parents stop interfering. The students actually do the reading; the parents don't do it for them. They can also do the math; but we often barge in when they struggle and do it for them (we call it help). Understanding what you really want is the key to defining the problem. Once the problem is defined well, the solution often magically appears.

2. What would a permanent solution look like?

I know we have discussed this previously, but it is important to keep it in order. Once you have the problem defined, moving in the direction of a lasting solution can really open your eyes to new possibilities. The paragraph above shows us moving from a well-defined problem to considering a lasting solution. I simply inserted the word 'permanent' into the defining question: "How can I permanently help my kids learn without it taking up so much of my time?" Thinking in this way allows you to look where you normally don't. Asking yourself how you can lose 20 pounds for the summer season is quite different from asking how you can weigh 125 pounds for the rest of your life. You may not find a permanent solution, but looking for it can keep you from the problem-soothing, symptom-treating, approach that keeps problems around.

3. What are the essential elements?

The essential elements are the key pieces involved in any problem/solution. In the process of creating a solution for a problem, it is important to avoid 'overcomplexification'. Overcomplexification is a word I adopted a few years ago to emphasize how we can include so much minutiae that we can't really understand what we are looking at. In this since, we can't see the forest for the pine needles. Getting your problem down to the essential elements is like understanding what makes water actually water. The answer is two hydrogen and one oxygen atoms. These elements combine to become H_2O, or what we know as the molecule for water. Problem-solving actually starts with that kind simplicity. If you have defined the solution as 'I want my kids to teach themselves', then what are the essential elements? Their schoolroom? No. Their SAT score? No. The essential elements are things like their capacity/ability, their skill-sets, the materials, and the process. There isn't much more to it. If they have the ability, the basic skills for learning information, adequate books/curricula, and a step-by-step process, then we know what to focus on, don't we? A permanent solution can be found in addressing one or more of these elements, or combining them in a unique way. If you have a good enough math curriculum, then doing just a few problems successfully each day will build them into self-teaching machines (if you don't do the problems for them). Read the instructions, do the problems, check the answers, correct your mistakes, rinse-repeat. Starting at a skill level that matches the curriculum means that they will continue to improve if you keep at it. A permanent solution is to have them figure it out; they keep reading the instructions and working the problems until they 'get it'. If the child does not 'get it', then do those problems over again (and again?) until they are mastered. Frankly, this is how they teach themselves the computer or smartphone. They keep trying different things until they 'figure it out / get it' and make it to the next level. A final tip is to work at picturing the elements and how they fit together in your mind. It's much easier to work with things you picture when trying to solve a problem or create a result. Again, focus on the various elements involved and don't overcomplexificate things! Simplify the elements. Think Ockham's Lever!

4. What are the 3 most obvious options?

In the same way that narrowing the elements allows us to think with greater clarity and precision, so too does limiting the solutions we want to consider. The principle in play says, "Limits yield focus." There is something powerful about creating a limit, whether it's a narrowed nozzle on a water hose or a deadline for a project. Water gets focused and efforts get focused. Brainstorming, for all its great press, isn't always all it's cracked up to be. If you get enough people giving you enough ideas, all you'll get is more confusion and less focus in the mire of possibilities. If you ask for advice from too many people you won't be able to decide much of anything. Sunlight is diffused, laser is not. Focus is birthed by limits. This principle helps greatly in our problem-solving efforts, so I suggest focusing arbitrarily on the three most obvious options. Edward R. Murrow observed that, "The obscure we eventually see, the completely apparent takes longer." Why not start with the three most obvious possibilities. Frankly, they are going to be in your mind anyway. There is something powerful about the number three with humans; the structure of a triangle, the beginning-middle-end of a story, and even the historic conviction of the Trinity in

Christianity. Even deciding you are going to make three points in a speech can be life changing as a speaker. Why wouldn't this work with problem solving AFTER you have completed the steps above? Since you have defined the problem well, and dismissed the reality pieces you cannot change, the options before you are probably pretty close to what you need to consider. Often these three ideas can also be recombined to generate other nuanced possibilities. There is also another version of the three options approach; consider the problem from the viewpoint of a scientist, an artist, and a genius.

a. The Scientist

The scientist solves problems by analysis and considering cause-and-effect. If you were a scientist solving your child's 'learn to teach themselves' problem, how would you approach it? I'd think through the steps of how teaching works and teach my child to follow these same steps. Teachers study the facts first, then they figure out the logic of how the facts fit together, and finally they decide on how to apply the theory to real life. Math, for example, has a lot of math facts (the addition, subtraction, multiplication, and division tables). They fit together in how they influence or affect one another ($10 - 4 = 6$). The logic of math makes sense when you know the basic rules (multiplying a number by its reciprocal always equals one). The practical application shows up in combining these things in algebra ($10x = 126$…so $1/10$ times $10x = 1$, and 126 times $1/10 = 12.6$…so $x = 12.6$). There's a little more to it, but not really.

b. The Artist

Artists make connections by means of images, sounds, and abstractions with an eye to beauty. They are looking at patterns and make connections others don't see. How is teaching oneself math like painting a landscape? Well, in a landscape you begin with the proportions; a frame of the land and sky and background colors. Next, you fill in the details and keep refining the picture. Math must work from foundational principles to refinements. So, if a student will learn the foundational principles, the refinements themselves will probably quickly fit into the 'picture' of higher math.

c. The Genius

Geniuses work in a slightly different way, often combining the skills of the scientist and artist. Their theme was summed up by Da Vinci, who observed, "Simplicity is the ultimate sophistication." The genius understands complexity in a clean and simple way. Teaching oneself math would come down to what Einstein's uncle Jakob told him when he had trouble with algebra (so the story goes). "As a child, Einstein's Uncle Jakob introduced him to algebra and called it "a merry science." He compared algebra to hunting a little animal. You didn't know the name of the animal, so you called it "x." When you finally caught the animal, you gave it the correct name" (sources vary). When you work out a solution as a genius you are looking for something so elegant that you exclaim, "Aha!" when you finally see it. What would be a simple 'Aha!' that could solve your problem?

5. How could I have a permanent solution with just one step?

I've told people the truth when I've said that my personal goal in problem-solving is to design a perfect system with a perfect result, which has only one step, and that step doesn't involve me! In this sense I'm employing the power of lazy. Why would I want to do anything in one step when I can accomplish the same thing in a half a step? When you have completed all the steps above, the next mental move is to see if you could do it even more efficiently. Homeschooling takes time in terms of grading math, writing, and reading comprehension. Jody and I wondered how we could do it in one step without involving ourselves? Eureka! We started having the older children grade the younger ones! This simple move did a couple of great things. First, it trained our older children to understand how their future professors might grade them (plus they felt like they were moving toward adulthood as 'teachers'). Second, it took a terrific burden off of us us 'teachers' concerning time. Our kids didn't want to spend their school day grading their siblings, so the learned how to be extremely efficient. Since the grades were recorded, we still knew we were on track academically with each of the kids. If you actually solved the problem you're facing with only one step, what would that step be?

6. Am I willing to think and wait for immediate certainty?

Solutions often come quickly and suddenly, but rarely when we are actually working on the problem. There are a variety of theories about why we suddenly have an insight in the shower or when we go on vacation. All I have been able to figure out is that our brain has to crunch the information and ideas we feed it over time. This sequence is (1) Hard Thinking, followed by (2) Patient Waiting. Somehow this process works beautifully. If you push too hard for an answer, your brain will tell you it's tired and needs to watch TV. If you don't do the hard work of thinking deeply about the problem at hand (using the steps above), then there is nothing much for your brain to work with. Working hard and then waiting patiently is the success sequence you're looking for (I promise). The fun thing about giving the problem a rest is that the answer often shows up as a certainty. What I mean here is that when it's right, you know it. There is an odd kind of 'I know for sure' when the right solution appears before you. If you arrive at an idea that you think might work and you want to try it out as an experiment, then most likely you still have work to do. Experiments are fine, but be patient and be sure if at all possible.

7. Can I explain why the solution should work?

If you can't explain it simply, you don't understand it well enough. –Einstein

Einstein's point here is that clear understanding leads to clear explanation. Often people claim they understand something, but that they just can't explain it. My experience matches Dr. Einstein's; I believe a muddled explanation is really a clear communication of a muddled mind! If you can't explain the solution, and why it should work, in clear and understandable terms, then it is safe to say you probably don't have a solution yet. Well, maybe you have a solution; but if you can't explain how it will work, then I assure you that you at least do not know how to make it happen.

8. Are there any unintended consequences this solution might cause?

At this stage you are starting to check out your idea, even if you know for sure it will work. Honestly, there are a number of refinements that we explain in our course on problem-solving; however, one of the important shortcuts is to see if something will happen that you didn't mean to happen. These kinds of consequences are sometimes hard to see, but they are also often avoidable. How hard would it have been for the Fort Worth library system to see that putting dollar bills in books (to get people to read) would easily lead to people rummaging through books for dollar bills and discarding them on the floor of the library? Frankly, not hard at all. At one point, we thought that allowing the kids to grade themselves in math was the easiest solution for time and learning. If we had thought it through, we could have guessed that it would have tempted some of our students to cheat, which they did! Doublecheck your idea by playing it out in your mind. If you implement your solution, what could accidentally occur that you'd rather not see happen?

9. What is the easy next step to implement the solution?

The final step in our problem-solving form is about getting in motion. The dirty little secret of getting results is that plans are often developed AFTER you get in motion. A major reason we don't solve problems is that we simply never try anything! There is a famous Confucius-type saying that asserts, "The journey of 1,000 miles begins with the first step." While that is clever, true, and valuable, I happen to have very tender feet. So, for me I'd say that, "The journey of 1,000 miles begins with putting on my sandals." The idea is basically that the next step is never hard. If you are facing getting in motion, but you can't find a way to do it; I'd say you are trying to do something out of reach. If you want to write a novel, the next step isn't writing the first chapter. The next step is turning on your computer. When you are relatively confident about your solution to a problem, getting in motion should be easy; but it often isn't. Why? You are over-reaching. Trying to get your young mathematician to learn ALL his math-facts is a big jump.

Why not knock out just four or five facts today? That's a good day on math facts. Tomorrow may be better, but not if it is too hard given your child's age, skill level, and environment. Some motion is great. More motion is amazing. But too much motion is sickening. The issue is simply motion, which can increase with sequentially small-but-better efforts. True? Finish your planning and start getting in motion. Ask yourself, "What is the easy next step to implement the solution?" That question will probably lead you to an action you can take before you turn the page. Good job!

SECTION IV

EFFECTIVE PARENTING

Chapter 14

Parenting: The Four Magic Common Sense Questions

In one of my earlier books, <u>The Absolute Quickest Way to Help Your Child Change</u>, I explained the core concept of setting up the parenting game to help your child change. For your benefit, I'm reproducing chapters 5 and 8 here for your benefit. I talk about God a bit more in this early work. My training in theology and my 25 years as a pastor come into play. If this is offensive, then please skip these chapters if you aren't open to a Christian view of these matters.

The Four Magic Common Sense Questions

Magic is intriguing. Whether it is the illusionist who awes us by making people 'float' in mid-air and objects appear from 'nowhere', or the possibility of changing a frog into a prince with a kiss; people love magic. Of course, in the Christian tradition we have been leery of magic. The battle between Moses and Pharaoh's sorcerers, the bizarre and magical pagan religions surrounding Israel, and the burning of magic books in Acts 19:19 add up to a strong case against magic. To use the word 'magic' in a chapter title is intriguing, but dangerous. Intriguing because we, as parents, would love to have a few magic questions we could use as a spell to change the destiny of our child.

Dangerous because too much faith in a technique or human notion can undermine the role of God in our lives.

If in parenting, you have hoped for this kind of magic over your child, then you will not find it here. There is a kind of magic though, for us as parents, in the wisdom of asking and answering four strategic questions.

Magic, in our sense, is not occultic or dangerous, but something that seems to have a supernatural effect because of the dramatic results it brings. It is not false to say that these questions are magic. Indeed, if you will give an honest effort to use them, along with the new understanding you've gained so far, you will be surprised at how dramatically and quickly your child can change.

One word of warning, however, as you begin to see just how capable you are of influencing your child's behavior; don't think you can perfectly control all of your child's actions. The very thing we have stressed all along is that you definitely can influence your child. This ability, however, is something to steward well, not something to abuse.

A SHORT REVIEW

We need to recall what we learned about the value of questions in Chapter 4. Questions are vital to help us think clearly about solutions. In fact, if you are not yet a common-sense parent, then the belief you hold and the questions you ask are the major hurdles for you. If you haven't quite embraced this idea, then re-read Chapters 3 and 4, marking with a colored pen everything that strikes you.

Two quotes from Chapter 3 are worth repeating: "The difference between common-sense parents and the rest is found largely in the questions they ask:' and "Right solutions follow right questions."

The value of these questions is that they will help you understand what is happening with your child, and what you can do to encourage change. If you are not seeing the things in your child that you would like to see, then it is almost guaranteed that you are not asking the right questions.

These Four Magic Questions are really just a starter kit that I have found to be helpful and common among effective parents. As you grow in your own common sense, you will add a few magic questions of your own.

THE FOUR MAGIC QUESTIONS

1. What do I see?

2. What do I want to see?

3. How is what I see being encouraged?

4. How can I encourage what I want to see, and discourage everything else?

These Four Magic Questions follow from our two

formulas: si? => ie! (See It? It's Encouragedl) and ei! => si (Encourage It! See It!). These questions will help you understand and use these formulas.

The four questions walk you through a process of thinking through your child's behavior from the problem to the solution, and they occur in a particular order. Moreover, there are two ways to apply these questions. First, you can apply them to your child's entire life and behaviors. Second, you can apply them to any specific problem or challenge.

Let's briefly consider the aim of each of these questions.

1. What Do I See?

This question is often the most difficult for many of us. It helps us to be objective instead of interpreting what is happening through our emotions or assumptions. For example, what do you see when you see a small child on the ground crying? Some of you see a hurt child, while others see a child crying for attention or for Mommy to pick him up; The only objective answer is that you see a child lying on the ground crying.

Instead of trying to at first figure out why something is happening, we need to simply focus on what is happening. Consider a few more examples.

Opinion: *What Do I Assume?*

"My child is arguing with me and showing me disrespect."

"My child is growing away from the family."

"My child is undisciplined."

Observation: *What Do I See?"*

"My child is answering my every request with a question."

"My child is hanging around friends I don't think are a good influence on him."

"My child is not turning in completed homework according to his teacher."

"My child is shy. My child hides behind me when meeting someone new."

There is a great need for us as parents to develop this skill of observation, because most of us are very unpracticed at just seeing the facts. We tend to rush to interpret them, often mistaking what is happening. With a mistake in the facts, what hope do we really have to solve the situation? Learn to simply and accurately ask and answer "What do I see?"

2. What Do I Want to See?

The power behind this question is that it gets us to develop a vision for our child's actions and life. It also moves us away from merely reacting to our children. In the middle of hurried lives and waning energy, most of us tend to "wait" for things to happen. Waiting on your child, though, only lets him run your home and ruin his life: "... *But a child left to himself brings shame to his mother."* (Prov. 29:1Sb).

We don't (or shouldn't) wait for our car to break; we keep it on a maintenance schedule. We don't (or shouldn't) wait for a job to come our way; we apply for it. The list goes on. We are to lead and develop our children, which require some idea or vision of where to go. Certainly we should discover and encourage the development of their own gifts and not our "dreams" for them. Dad who never got to play football, or Mom who never was a beauty pageant winner, should not try to live his or her dreams through the children. However, having a vision for their character and morals is exactly what Dad and Mom should 'dream' about.

By asking, "What do I want to see?" we can begin to focus on those things to develop in our child's life. We also get a clear picture of what desired behavior needs to replace the undesired one. Consider our examples again.

What Do I See?

"My child is answering my every request with a question."

"My child is hanging around friends I don't think are a good influence on him."

"My child is not turning in completed homework according to his teacher."

"My child hides behind me when meeting someone new."

What Do I Want to See?

"I want to see my child obey me or commit to obey me before asking any questions."

"I want to see my child keeping company with friends who are a good influence on him."

"I want to see my child turn his completed homework in on time, and have his teacher surprise me with a note about the change."

"I want to see my child stand at my side and politely say, 'Hello, I'm_____; it's nice to meet you.'"

There are no limits and no set of directions to this strategic question. There are many good books and resources for determining what kinds of behaviors you can expect from your children. My goal is not to tell you what your standards should be, but to challenge you to lead your child by setting in your mind and heart the behaviors and actions you want to encourage in your child. The best of all resources I've found is the Bible. A final warning must be added as you work with this question. Please don't limit your dreams to what you think is possible. Thinking, "But my child would never do that," only kills the power of Question 2. Answer it as though failure is impossible.

3. How Is What I See Being Encouraged?

The third of our Magic Questions takes us back to Question 1, but it goes a step further. This question helps us understand the behavior or actions we observe. Often it is difficult to see exactly how something is being encouraged, so don't give up. If you persist you will unravel the mystery of your child's behavior.

We are clearly assuming here that our principle of si? => ie! is true. If we see a behavior, then something is encouraging it. There may be exceptions, but they are rare. Let's re-visit our examples and fill in possible answers to Question 3.

What Do I See? How Is What I See Being Encouraged?

"My child is answering my every request with a question."

"My child is extremely curious and simply wants to learn." OR "I'm answering his question before he obeys, so I'm encouraging him to delay obedience by engaging in conversations with him."

"My child is hanging around friends I don't think are a good influence on him."

"My child is not turning in completed homework according to his teacher."

"My child hides behind me when meeting someone new."

"My child is getting more encouragement and support from his friends than from his family. Maybe they listen more while I lecture more? Maybe they hang out and I'm just in a hurry?"

"The teacher did not inform us of the problem for six weeks; therefore my child was getting away with it. Also, we have not been checking his homework each night before bed."

"When my husband pointed out that I always apologize by saying, 'She's our shy one,' I realized I've probably encouraged her to live up to that label."

These are just examples and there could be other reasons why these behaviors have been encouraged. The point is for you to begin to look for the cause behind the action. Answering Question 3 properly gives a great foundation to help your child change without your child's help.

4. How Can I Encourage What I Want to See and Discourage Everything Else?

This question is the most magical of our questions. This question begins to set in motion the innate gift within parents. It moves us to become our own experts for our own children.

Question 4 requires something you may not be very skilled at yet, brainstorming. The key is to simply get as many ideas as possible without criticizing or throwing away any of them. It isn't random, but an effort to list multiple ideas related to the action you want.

However, anything that encourages your child will work. As you study your child, you will begin to figure out how to answer Question 4, and continue to build a list of ways to encourage your child. Of course, the shortcut is to ask your child what he thinks will encourage him. You'll be surprised when he starts to give you some great ideas.

Encouragement is not the only part of this question.

Discouraging other behaviors and actions is also

important. A carrot can good and a stick can be too, but to use both in proper proportions is a powerful combination. The things to discourage are in the answers to Question 3. Let's look at our examples again.

What Do I Want to See?

"I want to see my child obey me or commit to obey me before asking any questions."

"I want to see my child keeping company with friends who are a good influence on him."

How Can I Encourage/Discourage?

"I simply will not answer a question until after he obeys or tells me 'I'm going to do it, but may I ask a question?' Also, I'm going to tell my child that he gets $5.00 every time he can get me to answer a question before he obeys."

"I need to work on my friendship with him. I think I'll begin to let him pick one activity each month just for us. I could also begin to provide activities, the car, extra money, or other encouragements whenever he spends time with some of his 'good influence' friends."

"I want to see my child turn his completed homework in on time, and have his teacher surprise me with a call or note about the change in my child."

"I want to see my child stand at my side and politely say, 'Hello, I'm _____. It's nice to meet you."

"The new rule will be Earn Fun with Homework. It will be homework first and fun second. Outside activities, friends, TV, etc., will be allowed after homework is completed. I'll also throw in a special treat when the teacher gives me that call or note!"

"We'll just practice until we get it right-first, in private, then as we meet people. I'll explain that 'This is my polite child' (not my shy one) and praise her as she follows the plan. I'm also going to have to have a serious consequence until she obeys."

Again, these are just a few examples. Please remember, you are to become the expert for your child. You are better able to figure out what will encourage and discourage behaviors in your child than any experts, books, or magazines. Don't be afraid to gather ideas from others, but usually the best ideas for Question 4 come from your own mind and heart; no one knows your child like you, nor can they.

THE EXERCISE

The most important thing you can do now is to apply these questions. It will take some work, but as soon as possible, you and your spouse (if applicable) need to sit down and answer these questions for each child. Ideally you should both read the book, but at least sit down and work through the Four Magic Questions together.

When I say work through each question, I mean to sit and answer all of these questions at the same time; and as fully as possible for each child. More children may mean more sessions, but it will be worth it. If this is overwhelming, then start with a small win. Pick a single behavior for each child and focus the questions on it. Appendix A may be copied or used to guide you through this process. Remember, you are seeking to develop and gain wisdom. The process takes time and isn't easy for any of us. Give yourself time to learn to observe and answer these questions. This is the most strategic battle to recapture your parenting gift. If you lose here, you'll lose. But if you win; what a victory!

When you do this exercise two important things will happen. First, you will create a new way to look at your child and her actions. What is more important, you will do this together, possibly becoming like-minded about your child for the first time. You can even throw the list away if you wish, because the impact of the exercise alone will begin to transform your perspective. The second thing that will happen, if you keep the list, will be that you will have a catalog of great ideas to help your child change. Someday it may even be a great gift to give your grown children as they begin families of their own.

Run That Play Till You Get It Right

One final suggestion will help speed up solving your child's issues; practice. In building a successful football team, practice is what counts. My coach used to say that we're going to run that play till we get it right. Guh! Over-and-over-and-over we'd run a particular offensive play until it was like clockwork. The same idea applies to becoming a master in the martial arts world. The martial arts commonly practice 'forms', which are a mechanical set of moves that can be applied to specific kinds of attacks or circumstances. In both examples, the point is that if something is practiced enough it gets into the 'bones', it becomes automatic.

You already know this principle and have probably used it often. When you set up a process or recipe for your kids to follow, you really want to practice it until they get it down. When adults, especially mom and dad were talking, we didn't want our kids barging in with a question. So, we simply practiced (yes, we made it a pretend situation and did it a number of times with each child) the child coming into the room and quietly putting their hand on our elbow until we stopped talking and asked them what they needed. This simple technique of practicing something in order to get it right is worth its weight in gold. Do you want the kids to hang up their towels? Have towel hanging practice. Do you want the kids to take tests better? Have test-taking practice (which is exactly what you do for the SAT/ACT). Do you want the kids to introduce themselves politely to adults? Then have 'introduce yourself' practice. The list can go on forever for both school and home related concerns. You will find that it works for two reasons. First, practice basically improves performance, no matter how well or poorly it is executed. Second, practice clarifies and explains exactly what you expect from your child. Clear expectations are what children need above all. Children should not be guessing about what is expected of them. Clear up the expectations and you'll usually see great improvement, guaranteed.

Chapter 15

The Absolute Quickest Way to Help Your Child Change

In the popular western, *Quigley Down Under,* the hero states while lost in the outback, "Don't know where I'm goin', but no use in bein' late." So it goes with our hurried lives. Our time is valuable. Our days are full. Anything that allows us to accomplish more in less time is instantly accepted as useful. No wonder a 'shortcut' is so attractive. If we can spend less energy and arrive earlier, we've beaten Time! So we think. But often, a shortcut is a gimmick at best, and a long fall at worst. There is a shortcut, however, to help your child change (for the better) without your child's help. It's not a parenting skill, but it is consistent with everything we've learned so far. It will also dramatically affect your child's life and behavior. You may, in fact, have skipped every chapter and opened straight to this one. If you did, you don't have to go back, but let me warn you; this principle is not for the faint of heart. This shortcut is powerful, but potentially difficult. This chapter explains the most influential power over your child's life, with the exception of God's direct work on the human heart. Without understanding the previous chapters, it will be hard to fully appreciate this ultimate shortcut. Also, combining this secret with all of the others we've looked at is the total effective parenting package. The greatest benefit will come if you stop reading here and start at the beginning.

What could it be that is so powerful over the lives of our children? Why are we just now getting to this principle so late in the discussion? What do we mean when we say it is difficult? Each of these questions and many more will come to your mind as you reflect on this shortcut to help your child change. Questions are good, but debating to keep from facing facts is not. Many parents who read this chapter may find feelings of anger, hopelessness, and frustration well up from deep within. Please don't see those feelings as a reason to put this book down.   Instead, be curious about your feelings. They are trying to tell you something. Learn to ask things like, "What is it in me that is so resistant to what I'm learning here?" If you can keep your objectivity as you are committed to learning, you'll find great hope. The truth really cannot hurt you, and it will help your child change!

Keep in mind that, "The only difference between a problem and a solution is that we understand the solution." Well, we face the same issue here. There is a solution available to parents that is seldom understood, but is often ignored.

Consider an example. She was about three when her parents decided to stop her from sucking her thumb. It seemed easy enough to discipline her for sucking her thumb, but soon she began to pull her hair out in little tufts. I was invited to help solve this dilemma, and we saw some improvement quickly. We simply tried to discourage the bad behavior as we've discussed earlier. After a short time, however, this little girl began to pull her hair out at night and carefully hid it under her pillow! We tried everything, but it just wasn't working. I personally thought we were taking a wise approach, but this little girl wasn't responding. When sound, common-sense practices don't work on a three-year-old, then you can be confident that something in the family more powerful than your direct actions is encouraging is encouraging the behavior.

That something is almost always the relationship between husband and wife, or mom and dad. A healthy relationship between mom and dad (however you conceive this) is the absolute quickest way to help your child change. But let me warn you again; though this shortcut is powerful (the most influential power in your child's life, with the exception of God's direct work), it is also potentially difficult, often ignored, and seldom understood. I'm warning you so you won't give up, not to keeping you from starting.

If you're a single parent, don't think this doesn't apply to you too. You may marry again, or you may still be seeing problems in your child because of enduring relationship struggles. But, why is this such a powerful influence, even a shortcut, to help your child change? The reason is simple and follows the underlying principle in this book – "If you see it, it's encouraged." The simple fact is that healthy marriages tend to produce healthy children, and less healthy marriages tend to produce less healthy children. Like breeds like. That is why, even if you are attempting to encourage the right things in your child, but are not living the right things in your marriage, you'll have little success in changing your child. You actually fall victim to the very thing you never liked as a child, "Do as I say, not as I do." If your marriage is healthy and growing, though you seldom properly discipline your child, that child will still have a better chance of turning out well than the child with parents possessing great skills but a sour relationship. The shortcut is to focus on healing.

How can you heal your marriage relationship? In fact, you may not even think much is wrong with it. The following is a simple test that will help you discern the health of your marriage.

1. Are you and your spouse more distant now or about the same emotionally as you were a year ago?

2. Do you or your spouse favor one child over another? (Just ask your children if you don't know)

3. Do you or your spouse feel the need to justify to an inlaw(s) the decisions or actions made by one or both of you?

4. Is anything or anyone (other than God) more important to you or your spouse than each other? (Include parents, friends, children, work, church, etc.)

5. For no medical reason, do you and your spouse come together sexually less than once per week on average?

6. Do your children think that every member of the family should be loved equally, including the

love between you and your spouse?

If you answer "yes" to only one of these, it indicates a potential problem in the relationship. More than one indicates even more serious problems.

The focus of this test is to look at how you as a couple see your relationship compared to the other relationships in your lives. The simple and common-sense truth is that health in a marriage comes when the relationship is elevated above every other human relationship. No child, friend, or in-law, is to be placed above the marriage. Moreover, no other relationship has more potential for true intimacy and closeness than marriage. It isn't just common sense; it is also part of God's original design for men and women. Consider the following passages from the Bible:

"Therefore a man shall leave his father and mother and be joined to his wife, and they shall become one flesh. And they were both naked, the man and his wife, and were not ashamed." (Gen. 2:24-25; All references herein are NKJV)

"So husbands ought to love their own wives as their own bodies; he who loves his wife loves him self. For no one ever hated his own flesh, but nourishes and cherishes it, just as the Lord does the church. For we are members of His body, of His flesh and of His bones. "For this reason a man shall leave his father and mother and be joined to his wife, and the two shall become one flesh." This is a great mystery, but I speak concerning Christ and the church. Nevertheless, let each one of you in particular so love his own wife as

himself, and let the wife see that she respects her husband." (Eph. 5:28-33)

There is a great deal we could learn here, but one thing is preeminent. The husband-and-wife relationship is to be special, separate, and unique to other relationships. It is to be intimate, loving, and respectful. It is to be 'a circle of two' that neither encourages nor permits any other relationship to compete with it. I believe, and many researchers and thinkers (experts) agree, that the greatest damaging influence on children is the failure of a marriage to maintain this standard. Further, the problems we see are largely encouraged by violating this God-invented, unique relationship.

Specifically, the phrase "leaves father and mother and be joined..." underscored the uniqueness and priority of marriage. First, leaving father and mother to be joined together elevates marriage above parental affiliations. Secondly, since our children someday will likely leave to be married, our relationship with them must come after our own marriage. It is the simple and clear design of God that marriage is to be placed above all other relationships. Even common sense befriends us here. What husband truly wants his wife to be emotionally closer to another person than she is to him? What wife wants her husband to be closer to a friend or his mother than he is to her? We are only emphasizing here what you know is true in your heart. Marriage is to be the unique-and-special human relationship above all others, and only the most cynical or hopeless would doubt it.

Why is understanding marriage as a priority so important? It is important because accepting the truth about marriage is a powerful beginning toward healing any husband-and-wife relationship. Moreover, a healthy marriage encourages the growth of healthy children. The simple fact is that the relationship between Dad and Mom is so powerful that few children ever overcome its influence.

If you understand our main parenting principle, 'if you see it, it's encouraged,' then you can understand what happens in the family. Each child has some very basic needs. He needs to feel safe. He needs to feel valued or significant. Safety and significance, however, must be balanced. No child feels as safe as when she is loved by a Mom and Dad who love each other. And, believe it or not, no child feels as significant as when her parents are most significant to one another. The sense of safety and significance directly flows from the relationship between the parents. When you and your spouse's relationship is stuck in the mud, what chance do effective parenting techniques really have? Your child simply gets caught in the middle, using her behavior to try to communicate with you. In her own way, your child could be trying to fix your relationship. She could be trying to get you both to act like a team by concentrating on her. She could be screaming about her own pain because of the screaming already occurring between the two of you.

Let's prove this point with your own experience. Think back over your own childhood. How close were your parents? Was it deep or superficial? Where they in turmoil? Was their conflict open or hidden? Do you remember how you felt the first time you wondered if your parents might get a divorce? Do you remember how it scared you, how you prayed in your own way that things would be OK?

You see, in your own childhood you knew intuitively that their relationship was profoundly important to you. If you only have memories of your parents' closeness, then be thankful and responsible to pass along such a wonderful heritage to your children. Common sense and the Scriptures both affirm that a healthy marriage is the shortcut to healthy children.

"But you ask, "Aren't there times when breaking up for the sake of the children is the best thing for them? You know, when there are irreconcilable differences? Keeping the marriage together only causes more pain and suffering for the children, leading to greater behavioral problems."

The idea of "breaking up for the kids" is a very old, and very misguided, default assumption. First, it would be worth your effort to read a *Reader's Digest* article titled, "Divorce and Kids: The Evidence Is In." In the article, Barbara Dafoe Whitehead documents the politically incorrect, but overwhelming, evidence concerning the effects of divorce on children. A more recent example of the toll of divorce is found in Jordan Peterson's video on The Price of Divorce and Terrible Relationships (https://www.youtube.com/watch?v=yMTqbc6L6BQ).

Second, and more important, the argument justifying divorce for the kids is actually an argument that doesn't think of the kids at all. What you could easily be doing is trying to justify quitting. Think about it. If you are really thinking about what's best for the children, then the option is clear: Improve the marriage! If you really love your children, do them the biggest favor of all, love your spouse / their other parent. Work on the marriage. It is the sure-fire, quickest way to help their behavior change. It is also the most fail-safe, least costly, least painful option.

Some statistics suggest that one-half of all marriages in the United States end in divorce. It is a painful tragedy and never should be approached lightly in any discussion. For a moment, though, consider the repercussions of a divorce. In an average situation where divorce occurs, both spouses could remarry. With a remarriage you suddenly have a set of complications besides the enormous financial cost over the coming years. Each of the marriages may bring other children into the family, which you and your children will have to learn to love. You may barely get to know these new children, and your own children have to figure out how to get along with their new siblings. Naturally, your children and the new children bring all of their behavioral problems together. Does your ex pay child support? What if a payment or two is missed? Your new spouse begins to resent having to pay for your deadbeat spouse's neglect. On the other hand, it may be that your new spouse resents some of your income going to 'that other person' who probably isn't spending the money properly on the children. Meanwhile, you can't fully enjoy your new relationship as you had hoped, because in the back of your mind you know that your new spouse has taken the kids and left before. You can't really be a parent to your new children because you and your new spouse can't fully be a team. After all, they are your ex's children. If you don't cooperate, they might leave. Your new spouse has made a decision that, "nothing is coming between my children and me. They're the most important thing in my life." This means that you will always be second to the children. What hope does that marriage have for intimacy? Worse still, all of this is further multiplied and complicated by the fact that there are still two more sets of families involved because of the new spouses' own previous divorces. And couples actually think it will be better for all parties involved if they get divorced!

If you think all of this sounds confusing, you're right. If you think it couldn't happen to you, you're dead wrong. With few exceptions, seeking to heal the marriage you are in requires the least pain and least effort, with the most promising results. Even if you think you deserve to be 'happy', happiness may be right in front of your eyes.

How to Heal Your Marriage

Many parents who read this chapter may feel angry, hopeless, and frustrated. Don't run away from those feelings; and don't let them stop you from continuing to read. Instead, be curious about your feelings. They are trying to tell you something. Many paths lead to a healthy marriage, but in our desperate days there are three crucial ingredients.

1. Quit Focusing on "Trying Not to Divorce"

While this may seem inconsequential, it is probably the most basic safeguard in any marriage. In order for a marriage to break up, a concerted effort to 'save' the relationship must have occurred. There are several important reasons this effort to save must happen in any break up. First, love or commitment of any kind insists that a couple can't merely 'quit' without a cause. In every relationship, getting to the level of marriage necessarily involves a series of wonderful moments and experiences that become the foundation for the greatest ingredient of a growing relationship; hope. The couple hopes for what the relationship can become together; in a sense, they are drawn together and toward the future with this hope in mind.

The first sign of problems in a marriage is seldom reason enough to quit since there is a reserve of hope available. Relationships end when they are seen as hopeless by at least one of the two. It is at the crucial juncture of admitting the relationship has problems that most couples make a fatal and very un-common-sense decision. They decide to "try to keep the marriage from falling apart." The decision is fatal. It will only lead to the final collapse of the marriage. If you think you have already made this decision, please decide right this moment to turn from it. Commit to never consider it in any relationship for the rest of your life. While this is really an issue of misdirected focus, there are other reasons this is a doomed-to-fail strategy.

The second reason couples start working at 'trying not to divorce' is guilt. Breaking up is a process of blame. The battle is between two former friends who are seeking to have the opponent carry away all the guilt for the failure of the marriage. Sometimes the relationship has drifted so far apart that there is a 'no fault' attitude. As the song goes, "There ain't no good guy, there ain't no bad guy, there's only you and me, and we just disagree." Songs and exceptions not with standing, most divorces have guilty and bitter people seeking to place the entire fault on one or the other.

A third reason to avoid trying not to break up is the need for a reason to divorce. Couples really can't move instantly from being in love and committed to ending the relationship. There must be a reason to end it. Working at not splitting up will help you find a reason by beginning a cycle of painful experiences that eventually outnumber the pleasurable ones. At this point a couple gets permission to end it. "We tried. It's just too painful. It won't work." And, so it won't.

The fourth reason is the most important one. The issue is focus. Whenever a couple begins to focus on not ending the relationship, they have turned their focus on the very thing they wish to avoid. I illustrated this point when I told you not to think about a moonlit lake, softly rippling in a warm breeze. Any effort to 'not' do something leads us to inadvertently focus on what we are wanting to avoid. Try an experiment right now: Get a watch or a timer and try not to swallow for 15 seconds. Really focus on not swallowing.

Unless you cheated by focusing on something else, you began to experience an overwhelming need to swallow. Indeed, you were probably more conscious and thankful to get to swallow than you've experienced in a long, long time. It is really simple. We become as we focus. A person who focuses on the negatives of the past becomes depressed. One who focuses on the possible negatives of the future becomes anxious. A person who vows to never be like Dad or Mom becomes just like them.

So, what happens when a couple focuses on 'trying not to divorce?' Divorce! If you want your marriage to improve, no matter how good or bad it is right now, change your focus. Refuse to use the 'divorce' word. Turn from 'trying not to' to 'trying to.' Make your focus improving the marriage. Commit to see how close two people can get before they die. Use questions like, "Are we closer now than six months ago?" or "What could we do together to make our love grow?"

The more you focus on improving the marriage, the further you get from even the possibility of divorce. At their fiftieth anniversary, I asked my grandfather how he and my grandmother lasted fifty years. "It's simple," he said. "We married for keeps." Maybe it really is simple. Every marriage experiences tough times and struggles. Successful marriage, however, focus on growing together and learning to see the struggles as stages of growth. It all begins with a decision and a constant focus. How close can you and your spouse get in this one life-time you've been given? Ask each other "Are you willing to find with me out how close we can get?"

2. Apply the Four Magic Questions to Your Marriage.

Remember the questions to apply to your child? They work for your marriage too. Try sitting down after a good meal at a nice restaurant and walk through these questions for your marriage or any areas of struggle (e.g. finances, communication, love-making, recreation, fixing up the house, laughing more together, dates, etc.). You may be shocked, if not a little embarrassed, that you both have created your struggles by encouraging the wrong things in your relationship. Ask, "In our marriage…"

- What do we see?

- What do we want to see?

- How is what we see being encouraged?

- How can we encourage what we want to see and discourage everything else?

If your spouse won't participate (don't guess, ask), then go through these questions by yourself. If you will apply them in the first person, then you will discover many ways to help your spouse change without your spouse's help.

3. Find a Supportive Environment.

What are the people you spend time with like? Are they making their marriages work? How do their children behave? Isn't it curious that you like your children to spend time with a good influence, but you don't do the same for yourself? Whether we like it or not, the fact is that we will become like the people we're around the most. Said differently, this may be the hardest step to follow, but you must find relationships that are successful in the areas where you are lacking or want support. To put it another way,

"You'll never be like the people you don't hang around." You don't have to give up your friends as much as you need to add some new ones. Just as in sports, you'll never improve your game if you only play against those who are only as good as you. Playing against better players encourages you to stretch. Spending time with people who are making marriage and parenting work will do the same.

So where do you find these people? The best bet is church, followed closely by your neighborhood or a homeschool co-op. The church is still the single most pro-marriage-success and pro- family-success organization around. If you don't like church it probably isn't church as much as it is a bad past experience. But all churches are not the same. Just as there are a great variety of restaurants in America, there are also a great variety of churches. It isn't a 'shopping expedition', but if you'll keep searching you will find a place to reinforce and promote all you hope for your marriage and children.

In our first church, for over the 19 years I pastored there, we only saw six divorces. We don't mean that divorced people don't attend, they certainly do. Nor do we mean that no one has ever left the church and gotten divorced. We mean that of those who have stayed and really sought to belong, we have seen most struggling marriages healed and transformed. We were focused on making marriages and families work, therefore we all worked together to encourage one another. In fact, we had a saying for newcomers: "You're welcomed to bring your problems, you're just not welcomed to keep them (unsolved)."

When you look for a church, find out if it is growing and offers help for marriage and parenting. A growing church with these priorities is likely the right environment. Also, and this should not surprise you, find out if it believes and teaches the timeless Word of God. Sadly, some churches really do not; it's a gem in the rough when you find a church faithful to the Scriptures. Of course, churches have struggles, but are they opening the Word of God for direction, or are they listening to the most resent fad? You will find that when you are teachable and well taught, you will change forever.

A WORD TO SINGLE PARENTS

All of this discussion may have seemed irrelevant to you if you are a single parent with no prospect of (or perhaps no interest in) a future marriage. How does all of this apply? First, realize that you have a challenge. One of the worst mistakes most of us make is to ignore the seriousness of serious situations. Second, don't despair. Most of what you've read can be applied. Specifically, you need to begin working toward at least an emotional reconciliation with your ex / the child's other parent. It is still deep within your child for his parents to 'get along,' even if they are divorced. Never mind if the other parent won't cooperate at first, follow the advice from the Word of God:

> Repay no one evil for evil. Have regard for good things in the sight of all men. If it is possible, as much as depends on you, live peaceably with all men. Beloved, do not avenge yourselves, but rather give place to wrath;

for it is *written, "Vengeance is Mine, I will repay,"* says *the Lord. (Rom. 12:17-19).*

Finally, make sure you compensate for the lack of a supportive spouse/ex with a healthy and supportive environment. There are other parents and friends and family members who can bring balance into your child-rearing. If you are not a good disciplinarian, enlist the help of others who are. If you are not nurturing enough, learn from those who are especially good at nurturing. Children were not designed to be prepared for life purely by the wisdom of one person, they need a healthy community to balance their growth. Please don't feel that you have to bring up your child by yourself.

CONCLUSION

So, what happened to the little girl with the 'hair problem' at the beginning of this chapter? As we sat down and worked through a few issues in the marriage, we discovered something very important. First, we found out that Mom favored the oldest daughter a little bit over the second one. Next, Dad favored the second daughter to make up for her being second. The rest of the dynamics are not important, since Dad and Mom committed to refocus on their marriage by making *their* relationship the priority.

These parents wisely sat down with the girls and apologized for communicating that everyone was on an equal par in the family. Dad explained that he loved Mom more than he loved the girls, but that he loved each of the girls in the same special way. Mom did the same thing, and both parents gave the girls permission to love Mom as much as Dad, and Dad as much as Mom.

Within a very short period of time, and without any further actions, the "hair pulling" of the second daughter went away and never returned. Also, just to press the point, the second daughter went up to her Dad the next day after the apology session and said, "Daddy, tell me again why you love Mommy more than you love me." She knew she was on equal par with Mom, which meant Mom and Dad's relationship was not the special one in that family [Update: The girls grew up to marry and have amazing families of their own!]

It is a plain fact, as illustrated here: When our marriage relationship isn't the top priority, it can literally make our children pull out their hair.

SECTION V

RESULTS AND MEASUREMENTS

Chapter 16

The 7 Outcomes of Your Successful Homeschool

Now it's time to focus on vision, or creating a clear picture of what you're hoping for as an outcome of your efforts in homeschooling. I don't want to underplay the importance of vision because there are few things actually more important in terms of organizing our actions and maintaining our motivation. If you don't have an idea concerning how you want your child to turned out, then how can you possibly organize what you're doing? It may be in your mind that we simply allow children to go according to their design and way, which is fine. Unfortunately, it doesn't have the same likelihood of desired results. Allowing more randomness into any system creates more chaos or undesired results. Human intelligence applied properly to a system creates order. Now you may be wondering how sometimes human systems are chaotic. It's not because of a lack of intelligence, it's because of conflicting interests. Usually, there are more than two sides battling or vying for dominance in a situation.

The curious thing about developing a vision is that we tend to first think we have a clear desire. Next, we picture what we want. Then we picture how to create what we want. Finally, we start executing or creating what we want. Not bad, but the truth is a bit more subtle and complicated. The reality is that as we picture what we want, our desire increases. So, the more we clarify the picture, the more we understand the picture, the more motivated we can become. Perhaps you've picked up a catalog at some point in your life and noticed there's a new gadget available that you never knew was out there. Suddenly you want something that you didn't even know existed until you saw it. It's very similar in that way. I believe love, or falling in love, is also in this pattern. We meet someone, we spend time with them, but as we picture or visualize what a future of building a life together with them might be like, we actually become more desirous, more excited, about all the possibilities of them and a life together. That is the nature of the game. In fact, this is how fear is removed or cast out. Remember, the Bible says that "perfect love casts out fear" (1 John 4:18).

So, in this regard, I'm trying to invite you to begin thinking about these seven areas that raising an independent student can influence:

The Academic-Ready Kid

For most of us, this is the chief concern of education. In other words, we want our children to be academically prepared for whatever they do in life. This is the nature of schooling and especially advanced schooling, such as college, master's degrees, and Ph.D.'s.

What would an academic or an academically-ready kid look like? It begins with the obvious fact that they are able to read, write, and do arithmetic efficiently. I remember asking my son, Tripp, what he most noticed about being homeschooled, compared to his friends at the University of Texas in Austin. I actually asked him this question at the beginning and at the end of his stay in college. Both times he had the same answer. He told me, "Dad, I noticed that I could read and understand what I read and interact about it in class; all my friends were amazed at that ability." In some ways, that is the most telling aspect of an academically ready kid. In other words, academics, the nature of the academy or the environment of learning around books and information and ideas and discussion, is especially connected to the ability to read. Reading as we know is able to connect us with the great minds in the world and in history. Writing helps us to communicate more effectively with one another. Writing also allows us to communicate permanently, because our writings can outlive our bodies. The third useful thing about writing is that it requires (or demands, or causes) us to think with far more clarity about any subject as compared to when we first begin before trying to write our thoughts.

An academic-ready child is going to be one who has those elements of being able to use her mind to think logically (empowered by the mathematics part), to articulate what she understands (empowered by the writing part), to grasp information from other minds (empowered by the reading part). However, to be academically ready also means that this child is able to function with such things as goals and deadlines and respect for others and discipline and character. In other words, all of the aspects of what it means to be ready for life are what come together for students to be ready for an academic pursuit. This may be part of the reason not all kids are ready for college. I certainly don't believe all kids should necessarily attend college, especially given the politicization of the academy these days. Nonetheless, if a child wants to pursue an academic career, there is no better preparation than learning to be an independent thinker. One who is able to understand, discern, and debate can think for herself; the ultimate antidote for manipulation, brainwashing, and outlandishly errant thinking.

The Practical-Ready Kid

The practical-ready kid is a student who's ready to put into practice the things he has learned. It's more than just simply being intellectually curious or a good learner or bookish. In the nature of practice, it means that one's understanding essentially can hit the pavement running. We see this missed all the time in human beings who are smart and informed about all kinds of trivia, but they don't know how to practically operate in the world. This practicality is essential for independence because it covers such things as handling bank accounts, driving vehicles safely, and negotiating through a problem with a purchase in a retail store. While these things may seem mundane, they are profoundly important for an individual to feel confident and independent. This aspect of learning is the ability to put into practice what you understand, and then function in a practical way. The practical-ready person in this world commonly has more focused energy than others. Once you know how to practically operate in the world with people and objects and information, you are not distracted by the stress and frustration of being confused about how things work. Your energy is directed to the things that matter to you so you can create the results you want to see in life.

The practical-ready kid understands how things work or she understands how to figure things out. Don't you want to develop a child who's an independent learner, one who is practical-ready? When we help them get practical-ready, we are not launching an individual into this world who is a drain on society, but one who is a practical contributor to what happens.

The Logic-Ready Kid

The logic-ready kid is especially, but not solely, connected to learning the essentials of mathematics. Logic is really about what makes sense, and often is not given to tight formulas because of its connection to human language; which of course tends to be a little more challenging than 1+1=2. When a child is developed into an independent learner who is logic-ready, he or she is able to look at a situation, a claim, a debate, or a news article and discern what makes sense (and does not make sense) inside of that article, for example. Of course, it doesn't stop with internal consistency, but rather it is measured in the world as well. For example, we have a current challenge with many aspects of history being framed as evil, when they were just matching the time. In other words, there are many things that have happened in history, during the period of time when the 'norm' then wouldn't be considered to be normal nowadays. It could be as extreme as issues like slavery or women's suffrage, but it can also be on the subtle level of what is seen as acceptable with the use of words.

In our day it is often demanded of us to have some respect for the challenges that are in play with different people groups in the use of language. American Indians should be called Native Americans and Chinese/Japanese/Korean's should be called Asians rather than 'Oriental'. The problem is when we look to a historical context that did not have such generic refinements in play. Each period was internally consistent, though there could be some bias involved. Adjusting our language is one thing, but to move beyond that and start condemning people for what they did in a context where it was not considered to be evil, is another problem. It is fundamentally irrational to condemn a different generation based on our morals and assumptions; to do so would demand that each of us would have behaved differently in that historical context (not possible!). When we are developing logic-ready kids, we are trying to help them think through the real logic of what was happening in the past in relation to what is happening now. Again, the best phrase is, "Does this make sense?" That's the question. We might as well condemn people for smoking in an era when they simply did not understand that smoking was harmful to their health; as my mother said, "We didn't know it was bad." Indeed, we might as well take down statues of doctors who thought that leeches helped heal, or that spontaneous generation was the cause of the life of germs (prior to Louis Pasteur and Ignaz Semmelweis). Would George Washington have ever owned a slave in our day? Would he have considered it an acceptable practice in our day? Clearly, no. So, how do we get ourselves to condemn a person by our current 'enlightened' standards? It makes us wonder what we are ignorant of that a few generations may condemn us for, true?

We live in an age where people are not very effective at thinking things through logically, largely because they are manipulated and untrained. People are often a part of a mob of individuals who are shouting one piece of rhetoric or a phrase about some heart-felt cause, without considering the complete story. The important thing a logic-ready kid does is to learn to look at both sides of the issue. When a kid is logic-ready, he is able to consider the other viewpoint and articulate it as well as his own. It is that posture that puts him in a position to be incredibly powerful and free of the whims and rationales of the cultural confusion caused by culture warrors. When we grow logic-ready kids, they become leaders because they can outthink the others around them. Of course, the goal is not simply to outthink others, but to draw everyone along to think more clearly, rationally, reasonably, and righteously as we work together to help this world. Perhaps the simplest value of being logic-ready, is that of being protected from being easily tricked; by salespeople, media, politicians, business partners, potential mates, etc.

The Society-Ready Kid

The society ready kid is one who is able to independently and effectively contribute to the world or society in which she lives. This, of course, will happen along the lines of her own talents and skills as she develops them and uses them in work or in civic contribution. The society-ready kid understands that society is a work-in-progress. In other words, societies have constant battles with trying to redeem areas where injustices prevail, while at the same time becoming more corrupt under the umbrella of individual rights. At the time of this writing, one of the curious examples is the legalization of marijuana. We have a culture that is violently, and increasingly, opposed to smoking cigarettes. The danger with smoking cigarettes for direct and secondary health issues is clear, and as such, it is common to have entire buildings and cities established as areas in which it is illegal to smoke. And yet, in the same exhale, the legalization movement is insisting that people be allowed to smoke marijuana. We live in a culture that is saying "smoke" and "don't smoke." By the way, marijuana smoke is as bad (if not much worse from a 'smoking' viewpoint) on the human body as cigarettes. The society-ready kid understands this kind of challenge and learns to think in ways that are both appropriate to interact with others and strategic in seeking a way to influence or change in a society.

So, when the danger such as concussions becomes clear in American Football, a noble individual starts working and cheering to have better protocols to protect that aspect of society. On the other hand, a society-ready individual would also not try to remove the individual rights of someone to play a sport he loves. Working at this balancing act with other skills, such as being practical and logical, is part of the burden and contribution of the society-ready kid. Protecting the society and guarding the individual are the tension points all society-ready kids must learn to appreciate.

The Emotion-Ready Kid

Growing an emotion-ready kid is in some ways strategically more important than any of the other ways we develop independence in our children. There have been times in our history, and it is still probably true, that every other hospital bed was occupied by somebody who was suffering from some type of mental or emotional problem. It is ubiquitous that health is destroyed by stress, relationships are destroyed by uncontrolled outbursts, and friendships are annihilated by passive-aggressive manipulation generated by hidden anger or fear.

When a child grows up to learn how to run his or her own emotions, then he is indeed ready to function well in the society. Individuals who experience failures in jobs or test-taking need the emotional strength to know how to get past their situation. Individuals who have relationships fall apart and are destroyed need to know how to emotionally understand and grow through that situation. The simplest aspect of emotional empowerment is to realize that we generally feel the way we feel because we think the way we think. The emotion-ready kid is one who is taught to gain insight through self-reflection and good thinking. She is an individual who can catch herself and think through what's going on in a circumstance so she can be freed from being emotionally compelled to meltdown or blow up.

Emotion-ready kids also are whole-hearted and vulnerable in their approach to life. In this way, they are authentic individuals who can be an incredible help to their friends and family members, to help them get good footing on emotionally challenging problems.

To understand the value of being emotion-ready, one need only watch the news for about thirty minutes to see how constantly emotional instability (and its bent to foster irrationality) is driving the rhetoric and confusion in so many areas of our society.

The Culture-Ready Kid

The culture-ready kid, similar to the society-ready kid, is one who is attuned to what's happening in the culture. In this way, a child is not simply a baby boomer or a millennial or a GenX, but rather, this person is largely independent of the culture because he understands the culture and his separate identity as an individual.

Culture is in some ways difficult to define, but is more-or-less an understanding of the accepted norms and beliefs (especially) within a given group. You always have a certain kind of culture on a sports team, in a business, and in a family. All of these separate cultures are about the recognized norms or beliefs for that group.

For a kid to be culture-ready means that she is able to understand the vocabulary of the culture, to understand the norms of the culture, but without having to hypnotically embrace them. Remember we're talking about independent learners; they can operate well within the norms, but they are not compelled to do so. In this way your kid is free. So, going to the symphony, for example, has a certain culture of how to dress and how to sit and how to behave. The symphony culture is different from the National Football League culture in terms of how to dress and behave.

The culture-ready kid is someone who is ready for influence, because he has been equipped to understand the game at hand.

The Spirit-Ready Kid

Honestly, this area is delicate and personal, but there is still something beyond the physical nature of human beings we call, "The Spiritual." Indeed, I believe it is important to honestly admit the spiritual nature of humans. This is important, whether we think the soul is the connection point between the head and the heart, or we understand the spirit to be the non-physical part of a human being that still can be identified as who we are; even if we have a particular eastern, western, or atheistic, or biblical viewpoint. It is not really my purpose here to insist on following my convictions. Of course, as a Christian and a pastor for two-and-a-half decades, I have a keenly biblical understanding of what it means to be essentially spiritual. It means to be vibrantly connected to God through Jesus Christ. That is the essence of what spirituality means in our own family. That being the case, we often speak in terms of 'how is your walk with God' or your 'walk with Christ', which means there is a connection to be in tune with God's will for life and purpose. In our family we are confident God is able to communicate, speak to, and guide our kids.

Nonetheless, it is also important that our kids come to their own conclusions, or rather their own convictions, about what it means to be a spiritual individual. In this regard, it's not a bad idea to expose them, when they're older, to a variety of spiritual expressions for their own understanding. Nonetheless, I want to insist that to develop a spirit-ready kid, you will want to teach them your own convictions. If you don't have any, then get some! Now it could be that they reject your view, but don't you want them rejecting what they clearly understand rather than what they clearly don't?

I believe one of the biggest mistakes we make as parents, one that does not prepare a child for life, is to avoid exposing them to any views at all; allowing them to meander through whatever their friends or the culture throws at them. Children need a solid foundation; and, if you are not a particularly spiritual person, the story may need to begin there. Your own understanding of spirituality will be a model and a guide for your child. The spirit-ready kid has something beyond the ensemble of academic and emotional readiness. This person has something virtuous and moral and deep within – and that makes the difference. I believe a child learning how to connect the deep core of his being to the Creator of the universe as a guiding foundation for solidly becoming an independent learner in this world is essential. But, that's my personal viewpoint.

Chapter 17

Motivation, Measurement, and the Limits of Influence

Motivation

Have you ever heard of the idea of single-point causality or the fallacy of the single cause? No worries, but it changes how you approach motivating your kids when you grasp the power of this insight: **Motivation always has multiple factors.**

How often have you said or thought, "My child isn't motivated." Or, "My child doesn't like _____ (math, writing, reading, etc.)." Not only do we say it for our kids, we make these claims for ourselves as well. What motivates us is not simple, but it is also not as complicated as you think. There are a couple of things you need to understand to step out into the light of learning how to guide your child. The two keys to motivation are understanding the Delta of Motivation (©Dr. Fred Ray Lybrand Jr.) and the difference between intrinsic and extrinsic motivation. In my book, The One Success Habit (You Can't Do Without), I explain extrinsic motivation as a basic structural issue in this way:

Why Does It Matter to Know Motivation Isn't Just One Thing?

Gaining the insight that motivation is about a relationship between what you want and what you currently have will dramatically allow you to focus on the success you want. In fact, there are really three basic elements in motivation:

1. What you want (the goal)

2. What you have (the current situation)

3. Time (a chosen deadline)

Motivation always involves all three of these elements. If you don't want anything, then you won't be motivated (but you might be happy). If you want something, but don't know you don't have it, you won't be motivated either (and you might be happy-though-deceived). If you want something and know you don't have it, but also think you have FOREVER to get it; you won't be particularly motivated to take action any time soon.

The key is to have a clear idea of

(1) What you want

(2) The fact that you don't have it; and

(3) When you will have (or create) it by

These three things, in a solid relationship with one another, will generate motivation. Said simply, it is a matter of the relationship between HERE, THERE, and DEADLINE. We can see this as the Delta of Motivation:

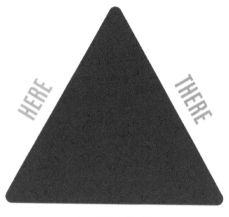

DEADLINE

Take a moment now and think about something you are motivated to accomplish. Aren't all three in place?

The 4th Element

Actually, there is another element that we can add to the Delta of Motivation. The fourth thing is a plan. The plan connects the other three elements together. We like to refer to it as the "path" that will take you from Here to There. Having a fair idea of how to begin is often the final missing ingredient for many people. Haven't you known what you wanted to do but had no idea how to begin? That's the issue sometimes. The plan needn't be perfect; it just needs to be something that is likely to get you to the result you desire. It is very much like *walking a path, along which you adjust the whole way around rocks and limbs and other obstacles. Just start with a plan that makes sense to you.*

All plans are adjusted along the way; so, don't overcommit to it, and please don't overthink it. Your delay, procrastination, and start-and-stops likely have more to do with a lack of a plan than anything else. Adding a basic strategy to the other three elements can often be the tipping point for action. And, of course, ACTION'S THE THING! Planning usually means you with paper, pen, and brain answering one question, "What do I need to do to make this happen?" Here's a complete view of the Delta of Motivation. Take another moment and consider something you want to be more motivated to accomplish. Are all four elements clear? Really? Work it out on a piece of scrap-paper and you'll see what's missing.

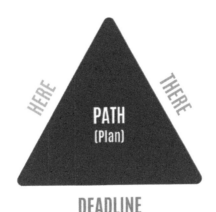

Realizing there are four elements involved in motivation is vital for the insight we need for ourselves and our students. When we get away from thinking that we, or others, are motivated by 'one' thing, we can begin to have useful insights into how to motivate others. It is as simple as it seems. One day, while we were including some friends' children in our homeschool due to a family emergency, I noticed a particular younger child not working on his math. He certainly claimed to be working on it, but it was at a pace of about one problem every ten or fifteen minutes. I simply asked him to show me where he was supposed to 'get to' concerning the number of problems he was assigned for the day. He showed me a number, let's say, "Problem 25." I then asked him, "Where are you right now?" He said, "Problem eight." I repeated, "You are on problem eight and need to go to problem twenty-five, right?" Yes. Then I said, "You need to go to twenty-five and are on problem eight, true?" Yes. I stressed this to establish a clear now-and-end set of points; a Here and a There. Next, I gave him a deadline. "I'm going to give you ten minutes to see how many problems you can get done, OK? OK. "Ready, go!" I said. When I came back, he had done four or five problems! That's the power of our pyramid of motivation. The challenges you face probably are around the issues of Here, There, Deadline, and Path. Just ask yourself, "What of these four things is missing for my unmotivated child?" Maybe it's all four.

Of course, there is another piece to motivation that we will call 'intrinsic' motivation. Extrinsic motivation is something outside of the child that is a motivating factor (Here, There, Deadline, and Path for starters). Another extrinsic motivation might be a reward, such as more free-time, video time, or extra ice cream. Intrinsic motivation is all about what your child may want or desire on the inside. The key is to get these things to match. A child's intrinsic motivation should match her extrinsic motivation. If you set it up that a child will get to go on a special fishing trip when he finishes his current math course/ book, but he actually hates fishing...well, it isn't a match. In this regard, you are the EXACT reason you are the parent, and the government and the grandparents are not! You are a student of your child, and you are to learn what kinds of things are really motivating both internally (intrinsic) and externally (extrinsic). It's unique to the child, and works best when they are a match.

Measurement

Yes, math helps with understanding absolutes and logic, both of which are very important. But, consider what follows (kudos to Peter Drucker who popularized some of these insights I've built upon). Whether it is your own homeschool, or your business, or your recent efforts at losing weight, here are the important principles:

1. If you can't measure it, it doesn't exist

2. If you don't measure it, you can't improve it

3. You get more of what you measure

4. What you measure moves you

5. Your measure is your mission

6. If you measure wrong, you'll manage wrong

The first three principles come from Dr. Drucker and the medical/engineering communities, while the last three principles are from my own observations while coaching organizations. Drucker was a noted management thought leader who turned his final years of focus to helping non-profit organizations. The medical research community, legitimate statisticians, and savvy engineers all contributed the important third point. The essence of their point is that measuring creates a kind of focus upon, and admission of, reality. Reality is what we really have to work with if we are going to be practical at all. When we bring attention to what is actually going on, then there is an increased likelihood that things will improve or grow in that area. From my experience in the 'church world' over the decades, I like to pick on my friends, the Baptists, to emphasize the point. What do Baptists measure? OK, so think about it...

Example: Baptists historically tend to measure baptisms. Maybe they have backed off in recent years, but it's properly in their name. For decades they reported to the regional or national offices the numbers they baptized (per church / district). This focus on baptism meant that they subtly, or not so subtly, were being encouraged to focus on baptizing more people. Occasionally this can go awry, with not a small number coming up with ways to encourage 'rededication' and 're-baptism' to match the crying need to report the numbers being measured. Please don't misunderstand my point as an attack.

One of my books (_Preaching On Your Feet_) was published by Broadman/Holman Academic (Baptist Press).

I'm sharing this because I am inviting you to understand the practical power of math and measurement. In your own homeschool, if you simply record the number of pages read each day, you will almost guarantee more reading. If you record each day the number of math problems worked and the overall percent correct, you will all-but-guarantee improved math scores. Using math in our homes and organizations allows us to look at measurement in very honest and profound ways. Knowing math actually allows individuals to become great motivators and persuaders in the day-to-day world. One of the non-profits that hired me to help them get more organized and more effectively raise donations had not charted the money received monthly compared to the money spent monthly — for 15 years! It is easy to sound judgmental, but the problem is that a smaller ministry is busy doing the work, so things can get neglected day-to-day (which then can quickly add up to years). The truth is that once we had them measuring things, they were instantly and massively motivated. Why? Well, it's simply that they suddenly understood what was going on! This is why measuring your own children's math/reading skills can have a powerful effect. I don't like measuring children too early, since it's easy to label them as 'slow' or 'behind' in the early years, when it frankly isn't true. On the other hand, it is important to start finding out how things are going (at least by age 12, in my view). If a twelve-year-old is behind in reading or math, then you are at a good place to start tweaking the process to improve things.

Yes, math helps us measure things. When I, however, add that your 'm is your mission', I'm saying that you need to have integrity. If you are committed to having an educated child, but you only measure their happiness (or their success in sports, etc.), then something is amiss. Measuring how they are really doing academically gives you the clarity you need to improve things, and it gives your students confidence as they can see they are getting better. Additionally, if something is genuinely amiss with their ability to learn, it allows you to see it early; well before it's too late. One of the most distressing things for me is to see parents avoid dealing with issues in a timely manner. You are already measuring something anyway, what is it? Is that where you want to head? Is that your mission? I'm hoping you'll start measuring progress that really matters, and then make the needed adjustments.

Another power of measurement is its predictive nature. Wouldn't you like to know the odds are in your favor? Income and budgeting are easy examples of measuring's value. If you are in a business that doesn't have a steady income stream, measuring these areas month-to-month allows you to account for fluctuations and take appropriate actions. A friend of mine was an owner of a Chick-Fil-A in a shopping mall many years ago. One time he mentioned that more than ¼ of his income for the year came from the period from Thanksgiving and New Year's. That's a nice thing to know. You'll need to make sure you have saved some money for the slow periods in the year. Staffing needs will go up, so hiring for the holidays becomes a must-do. Enduring through the season is easier because your metrics tell you that it won't last forever. Churches go through the same challenge with giving being down in the summer and over-the-top in December. Things just don't happen in even numbers, but patterns do show up if you keep up with things. Moreover, knowing the metrics can simply boost your confidence. While it can be hard to get at the perfect numbers, on average homeschoolers consistently

✓ Do better on standardized tests than non-homeschoolers

✓ Score higher on the SAT than non-homeschoolers

✓ See about 10% more homeschoolers graduate college than non-homeschoolers

These numbers may change or be debated, but at the very least they tell us that homeschoolers, generally speaking, do no worse than non-homeschoolers. True? In my research and experience, it is the power of learning how to become an independent learner that makes the difference. Students trained in a mass education structure are going to be especially influenced by the crowd they are around and the guidance of the teacher. One of our friend's sons went to a major Texas University and was flunking because he couldn't understand anything the chemistry professor was saying due to style and language challenges. This young man wasn't alone, because most of the class was failing. He gave up on class-time and just studied the textbook as a self-teacher, finally getting the highest grade in the class.

How to Measure

Measuring isn't difficult if you are willing to keep making adjustments until you are happy. Most of life is learning that you can't start with perfect. So, how do you measure? Just like measuring the height of your child, you just need a combination of distance and units. With a tape measure you can find out that your child is sixty inches (five feet) tall. The unit you are using is inches. The distance is from the floor to the top of his head. Sometimes there is depth (measuring a waist if you care about three dimensional things), but distance and units will normally be enough. Is it any different with math or reading or household maintenance chores? No.

Measuring math is a matter of the total number of problems to complete (distance) and the number of problems that are correct (units). Time can be a factor, but in math it is still about the number of problems that a student is to complete in a certain amount of time. In our case, we measured the number of problems correct out of the number of problems we expected our kids to complete within two hours of math. The number of problems expected changed based on whether or not they were consistently getting 90% or more correct over a two-week period. If they were consistently below the 90%, we reduced the number of problems. [Aside: It is vital for you to have the conviction that it is better for a child to master ½ of his math by the end of high school, rather than completing the entire math program without really understanding math at all. Math is not a subject that is given to 'I'll figure it out later as I keep doing it' kind of subject. Reading can work that way as we get more details later in a book, but not math. Mastering each principle or formula in math is absolutely necessary to move on and master the next one. Please do not let your child move along to the next math subject; that's what schools often do! Slow down and learn...speeding up will come in due time with confidence and know-how.]

Measuring reading is a matter of pages or chapters (unit) over a certain time period (distance). We had a target for the number of pages a child was to read over two hours of reading time. The easiest thing to do is to have your student read three pages of the book and see how long it takes. Use that number as a baseline for the number of pages you expect. We usually made the number of pages about twenty percent less than what they 'probably' could read in a two-hour period each day. We wanted to be fair, and we wanted to reward them with a few minutes break if they buckled down and read their book with focus. However you choose do it, knowing the number of pages read each day can reveal great patterns and motivation for adjustments and confidence. Comprehension itself needs to be measured in another way, which is commonly what tests are about. We found that having the kids explain what they read to each other each day (about five minutes) was a solid approach to keeping comprehension in the forefront. Thank you, Charlotte Mason!

Chores work the same way. We renamed them 'household maintenance' and simply had chores assigned (units) to be done within a specific time period or by a specific deadline (distance). It is common for moms to become the 'reminder' (aka nagging) of what needs to be done. This is such a waste of time and energy. Just make a chart and put the kids and the chores they are to do daily/weekly on it. Post it on the refrigerator and have THEM fill it in each day. It will work like magic, I promise.

A slight tweak could be in order here concerning the notion of distance. Distance is not the only thing to measure, but it is a great way to think about it. Quantity and quality are also legitimate things to measure as well, so 'how much' or 'how good' are certainly acceptable. In educating our children, it is still important to note that we are concerned with growth, or improvement, over time. This 'over time' idea is embedded in the use of distance as a measure. Here's what can make the difference, "Look where you were. Now look where you are!"

Limits of Influence

It's almost unfair that we've been given the charge of growing our kids, but without the full range of power needed. How much can you really influence, control, or guarantee your child's choices and success in life? This is a very important question, but it follows just behind another one: Should you try to influence, control, or guarantee your child's choices and success in life? Most of us are kind of a GOD 0.5 in the way we operate. One-half-a-god means that we often think we know exactly how the universe should work, but we don't have the power to make it happen!

Clearly our influence as parents starts out strong. Even if we don't exercise much control with scheduling and feeding, the baby still can't force us into sleeping all day and staying up all night. Even in the most painfully lax homes, eventually the influence of the parents, friends, sun, and moon win out. Of course, exercising influence in the early years cultivates safety, use of language, hygiene, manners, intellect (connected to vocabulary), and a whole host of other important things for life. While influence can start out strong, our babies grow up and display the anti-influence weapon of mass destruction; the WILL. Human beings are not dominoes lined up to dutifully knock the neighbor down on the way down themselves. With human beings, your students, the dominoes can move.

I only mention this because you really want to come to grips with this important fact; you can't guarantee the future. You can't guarantee what your kids will do, who they'll marry, and even if they'll want to have much to do with you. It isn't that we can't influence our children, we certainly do; but it is important to know that our influence has limits. It really is their life to live, not yours. It is really up to them to succeed or fail, and even then, they cannot guarantee their own future. There are simply limits to what we can control in this world. Controlling everything is God's business, so when we fight reality, we are technically fighting with God.

Alas, all is not lost! Some years ago, I studied how commodities investing works (talk about something you can't control!) and ran across a simple idea borrowed from boxing, "The biggest and the baddest doesn't always win, but that's how you bet." Yes, it is about putting the odds in your favor; it's as simple as that. If you read a lot and read a lot to your kids, what would you guess their interest in books and reading will be over a lifetime? If you are involved in a good church and have close friends in your faith, what are the odds the kids will follow that path? What if you are a top athlete and immerse your kids in that world, is there a chance they'll follow that path? The truth is that it is common and understandable that our influence can guide our kids by introducing them to a particular approach to life. Our influence is also a way to give permission to our kids. It emotionally tore me apart to write my first book, my kids have now written twelve books among themselves (and countless blogs and articles). You definitely have influence by example and creating the context of learning and life. However, you also definitely cannot guarantee the outcome. Be wise, but be realistic, and things will go in a good direction…I'll ~~guarantee~~ bet on it!

SECTION VI

THE REAL SECRET OF

INDEPENDENT HOMESCHOOLING

Chapter 18

It's Not Your Method, But Your Mindset That Matters Most

I think it's undeniably true that the human brain works in models. The trick is to have your brain work better than the other person's brain because it understands the most fundamental models --- the ones that do the most work.

-Charles T. Munger (Billionaire partner of Warren Buffet)

Whether you skipped ahead or made it this far, congratulations! I know you probably skipped ahead, so feel free to read this first. There is nothing more practically powerful for your students, family, marriage, and life-work than your mental models. I know this sounds heady, but I promise you we can't possibly get more practical. Impact really flows from a mindset in the moment you act, but it is the mental model that is behind your mindset. Practically speaking, they are both the same thing.

Even though I've offered many methods and tactics here, my entire hope has been to help you tweak, adjust, enhance, and even change the way you think about home education. I've tried to sell you on the wisdom and power of growing independent students, and how this understanding will impact the world for good.

Let me illustrate the point by discussing reading for a moment. There are two major methods to teaching reading, one of which has thankfully diminished over the years. In 1955 Rudolf Flesch wrote a book called Why Johnny Can't Read to address this issue and return phonics to the American classroom. While the controversy continues, most homeschoolers have championed phonics as the best means of learning reading fluency. There are two ideas (mental models) behind the two approaches. In the phonics model, the idea is that students are taught the component parts of a word so they can 'sound out' any group of letters (a word), and so learn to read. This model predicts that knowing the code will allow the student to decipher any written words they encounter. The other model is known as a whole language (look-see) model. The idea behind this model is that humans use their prior understanding to construct meaning. In this approach, students are basically taught to read whole words, rather than look at the parts of the word. The whole language approach also has a self-esteem goal in mind; they often want the student to feel like they are really reading rather than learning meaningless symbols by rote.

Without getting too deep into the debate, I believe phonics is far superior because it is actually unravelling the code 'linguists' used to create the written word. Whole language can hinder a child by limiting reading to 'known' words alone. Furthermore, there is plenty of evidence that it can lead to learning disabilities, etc. For a thorough argument, please read the following article from Learning Disabilities Online [http://www.ldonline.org/article/6394/]. It is common to have a third mental model which blends the two, but it too is found wanting. Learning phonics kicks in a whole language answer in the due course of time. The gap in learning phonics, to when a child can read, is easily bridged by reading good books to the child and asking them to occasionally repeat the basics of what they were just read.

Now, to our point. The model of how children learn to read gives rise to, or dictates, the method used. Frankly, if you believe in the whole language model, then you will quit using a phonics method in the due course of time. The same thing applies to discipline, parenting, house cleaning, playing sports, learning mathematics, personal hygiene, how much makeup one wears, and the host of anything-and-everything that comes down to some method. **It's not your method, but your mindset that matters most.**

In teaching our first child to read, we had a phonics program for him to work through. Subtly and secretly, Jody began to introduce whole language sight words into the mix from her old college materials. Jody has both a B.A. and M.A in Early Childhood Education, and was steeped in whole language theories. Even though she intellectually accepted phonics, her mental model still included whole language ideas; therefore, it couldn't help but creep into her method. Her best memory is that she felt like our child needed more 'sight words', so she substituted learning phonics with learning sight words (which slowed down the learning process dramatically). Your exact problem will be the same with anything you do in homeschooling. If you buy a curriculum, but don't understand and embrace the model behind it, you will eventually change or abandon the curriculum as 'it doesn't work' for our family. Again, this book you are reading is about helping you to thoroughly understand and embrace a mental model for growing independent learners. If you don't accept the model, you'll never follow the method. In fact, you would do well to quit looking for methods. Instead, think long and hard about how to best help your child learn and prepare for life as a happy adult! The following points will give you a good start in forming your own mental models.

- ❑ **Mental Model Defined**

- ❑ **Humans Are 99% Reactive**

- ❑ **Reactions Are Based on Choices**

- ❑ **Choices Are Based on Mental Models**

- ❑ **Mental Models Interpret Reality**

- ❑ **The Lybrand Mental Model of Behavior:**

    Results come from Actions; Actions Come from Choices; Choices Come from Reacting to What Your Mental Model Sees and Predicts

Mental Model Defined

You may study all of this on your own, but I want to offer a practical shortcut by sharing with you what I've learned over the decades. I'm not offering a scholarly paper, but simply the way I have come to understand these things so far. If I'm plagiarizing, it is 100% an accident as I simply don't remember where I was introduced to some of these ideas. As far as I know, these are my own conclusions, but I'm not alone in this understanding.

Wikipedia says, "A mental model is an explanation of someone's thought process about how something works in the real world." That's okay, but I think they are missing that when a model is engaged, it really has to do with the future. I offer, **"A mental model is simply a way to think that predicts what will happen in the future, given a situation or set of circumstances."** Maybe they are not so different, but I want to stress to you that this is all about taking action based on how you are predicting things will turn out. A model is explaining how something works in the real world, but doesn't it find its usefulness in the future? Computer modeling of hurricanes is a good example, even though they aren't very accurate more than a few days out. Hurricane modeling is a method designed to especially predict landfall. Based on where a hurricane lands, precautions and evacuations will be in order. In educating your child, the same kind of thing is in play. What does a student need to know to be ready for life? What skills do they need? If they are wanting to go to college, is that a different game than going straight into the workforce? What about a child's unique interests? How does all of this fit together to choose actions *now*, which will make things turn out well *then*?

You can already see that your predictions will tell you how you need to act now. If a child cheats while young, it might suggest they'll cheat worse in the future. While this isn't guaranteed, the mental model about cheating will tell you what to do now for the future. If your model says gaming all day in a dark room won't matter, then it isn't a big deal. If your model predicts a child needs to learn to be socially skilled with others (and get some outdoor exercise), then your actions now will not support full-time gaming.

One of the nice things about the Reading-Riting-Rithmatic model is that it predicts good things in the future for your child. If they can read and write and do math, then they are equipped with terrific skills for learning almost anything. They can acquire knowledge from others (reading), problem-solve with the language of science (math), and refine & articulate their thinking as they work with others (writing). You already have all kinds of mental models for all kinds of things, but now you can direct some of your destiny by improving and adding the models you need.

Humans Are 99% Reactive

Even as you read these words you are proving the point. You react to seeing letters in a certain order, which means you react by seeing words, which means you react by seeing words represent full thoughts, etc. When you see something you agree with, you react with some kind of affirmation. But, when you see something new or challenging, you react with thinking through your experiences and predictions about how things might change if you accepted this new idea. The phone rings and you react. The server comes and asks for your order and you react. You see an attractive person, a dangerous person, or a mysterious person; and, you react.

At the most basic level, the reason we are wired to react to everything is because everything is connected. Most of these connections are experienced very indirectly, so we seem to be making choices all the time. Indeed, they are choices, but not really stemming from willpower. One mental model I use frequently is to assume that people are taking their actions because they have no other legitimate choice in mind. They may have several options; however, one is better than all the others. So, why would someone ever take the less-than-best option they see? They wouldn't, period.

At this very moment of writing, Jody and I are waiting until the top of the hour to facetime our granddaughter who lives many states away. Arranging a time has been a series of negotiations between her schedule and our schedule; this includes her nap, my run, her parent's date at the park with friends, and our dinner out tonight. Add to that the desires we have to connect and to make everyone happy. It's complicated! Yet, with a series of back-and-forth reactions, we settled on a time and it will probably all work out. Just keep in mind that everything is a sequence of actions and reactions to those actions. That admission will get you ahead in the game of life, and especially, in your homeschooling independent learners.

Reactions Are Based on Choices

Perhaps this is a little redundant and I'm splitting hairs, but engaging a reaction is still a choice. As mentioned earlier, the choice is one of a few available. Of those few that are available, the one seen as the 'best' is the one that is finally acted upon. Human beings are thinking-feeling-acting things, but the heart of it is still a choice. Knowing this comes in pretty handy because you can then start predicting how people might act, including yourself, in any particular situation. For example, have you ever seen someone who is struggling to make a decision one way or another? Frankly, you've probably experienced this yourself quite often. Why? Why would it be hard to make a decision if we are simply reacting to things that are coming at us? The answer is pretty easy to discover once you can admit that 'not choosing' is also a reaction. Not choosing means that your best choice is to make no choice at all, which is still a choice. We don't want to deny that we are making choices, what we need to get out of our head is the odd notion that we aren't choosing when we are reacting to what's going on.

In the homeschool world at your house, you are still fretting over choices of curricula and daily schedules based on what all you believe is available to you; based on how you think. It's not that you aren't choosing, it's that you don't have a good way to think about the choice. Now that gets down to your mental model. Your mental model is the basis of all your reactions, of all your choices.

Choices Are Based on Mental Models

Now, this is where all of our hard thinking gets fun! Why do we choose what we choose? Specifically, how does it work? The obvious point is that our mental model [N.B. There are actually innumerable mental models each of us has constructed and embraced. It is commonly referred to as a lattice of mental models. The idea is that many of our mental models touch one another; and so, there are layers of influence in the models we hold]. So, what is happening is that an event of some type comes into view, and our model tells us immediately what options are available. Next, our model for deciding comes into play and we pick the ONE CHOICE that makes the most sense; or specifically, the one model that feels the best to us. For example, think about something as ordinary as birthday cake at a birthday party. Even if you are on a diet of some kind (which is also mental-model based), if your view of how things work includes not being seen as rude, celebrating with others, and having cake is a special treat I deserve and don't want to pass up, then the choice of having a piece of cake becomes the obvious thing to do. If you didn't have those ideas in mind, you might have other ideas in mind, like 'I ate too much lunch, sugar will hurt my diabetes, cake always makes me feel bad later, people don't care what others eat', etc. With these in mind, your obvious choice is to skip cake at this time.

Finally, it can get a little more subtle; you can have another mental model that says eating a sliver of cake is OK, but eating a large piece is gluttony and debauchery! In this case, you might have a small piece of cake, if you also have it in mind that people are laughing about how little you are having is okay.

How does this relate to homeschooling? It relates because you have a lattice-work of mental models that dictate the choices you react with every day. How do kids learn math? Can any child learn math? What is reading about? Does it matter what a child reads? What do you think about scheduling? Are children to be encouraged to be free spirits and study when they'd like? Do children work best with assignments and deadlines? All of these questions simply reveal parts of your own mental models. The way you think about these things and how they work, along with what you think they predict about your child's education, become the basis of your choices for homeschool. Everything this book is about is aimed at helping you shape your mental models so that you can make the right choices (reactions) for the outcomes you want for your child. **It's not your method, it's your mindset that matters most. There is honestly nothing more practical.**

Mental Models Interpret Reality

In 1982 the findings of medical researchers revolutionized the treatment of stomach ulcers. Up until that point, doctors simply misunderstood the actual cause of these ulcers. In those days, a patient would come to the office and it would be clear that there was a hole (ulcer) in their stomach, which created serious pain and discomfort. Stress was the 'culprit' in combination with lifestyle choices. Obviously, doctors would prescribe something to reduce acid and exhort the patient to de-stress, rest, and change their lifestyle. Makes sense, right?

But then, in 1982, a new model of ulcers arrived; ulcers are caused by the bacterium known as helicobacter pylori. Yes, some ulcers are caused by too much aspirin and ibuprofen, but it really is the bacteria that are the culprits! This led to a treatment of antibiotics plus bismuth subsalicylate (Pepto Bismol). Veterinarians had been using this combination for decades for the same problem in pigs, but until 1982 millions of people needlessly suffered.

This is a stark example of a mental model dictating behavior. Please don't miss the point; if you misdiagnose how children learn and what they need to learn for life, you will follow a method that will steer you off course. First, there is a shout-out to medical science, which can keep learning and improving. Second, we need to realize that the mental model kept interpreting reality inaccurately. Imagine being a pre-1982 doctor. A patient comes in and you discover that they are incredibly stressed out in life. You also discover that they have a hole in their stomach. At that point, since you also believe ulcers are caused by stress, you recommend to your patient a lifestyle change along with some symptom-calming medicine. Your mental model is actually guiding you to misinterpret reality. The patient is stressed BECAUSE of the ulcer, it's not that the ulcer is caused by stress. Sadly, there are doctors today who still use the old model.

In your home and homeschool, you are constantly tempted to interpret what's happening based on some mental model(s) you are using. If you think children will naturally go to bed and sleep when they are tired, then you will see your late-night child as a 'really active' toddler. That will likely lead you to try to 'tire them out' (or sedate them with a lot of milk or food) in order to get some sleep. If your mental model is that children need rest, even if they don't sleep, you'll see your toddler as not yet trained to go to bed and stay in it for the night. Here's a list of questions that should make the point clearer about homeschooling:

1. Do you see a child who can't learn math, or a child who hasn't yet learned math?

2. Do you see a child who is a poor speller or a poor guesser?

3. Do you see a child who is a free spirit, or do you see a child who doesn't obey boundaries yet?

4. Do you see a child who is hyper-active, or do you see a child who needs some physical play time?

5. Do you see a child who is a picky eater, or do you see a child who isn't hungry enough at mealtime?

6. Do you see a child who hates reading, or do you see a child who hasn't yet discovered the joy of reading?

The list could be endless, but it gets at the point that your theories (mental models) about how life works, cause you to interpret what's happening in a specific way. You will dramatically advance as a Chief Learning Officer if you recognize that your mental model may be playing tricks on you. Learn to ask, "What would someone who thinks differently about this think here? How would they interpret this behavior or challenge?" This way of thinking (yes, it's a mental model) will help you see more accurately and more honestly; which means you can make better decisions as you tweak your own understanding of how homeschool works. Now, let's put it altogether.

The Mental Model of Behavior:

Results Come from Actions; Actions Come from Choices; Choices Come from Reacting to What Your Mental Model Sees and Predicts

There it is, our whole model. *Results Come from Actions; Actions Come from Choices; Choices Come from Reacting to What Your Mental Model Sees and Predicts.* Another way to view it is to see that we (1) Have a mental model; which then (2) Sees what is relevant and makes a prediction about how the future will unfold; which then (3) Causes us to react by making a decision; which then (4) Directs us to action; which finally, (5) Produces a result. Clearly there are many nuanced details in here, such as the fact that your reaction involves how you feel. Attempting to feel better (or less bad) means that actions are motivated by what we think will make us feel good. However, this is still a reaction largely based on our mental model(s).

What's next? Well, the result caused by taking action is something that our mental model will move us to repeat the process and improve it (most likely). Wash, rinse, repeat. It's important to note that since this is the process underneath your reactive life, the 'goal' you try to set may have no impact at all. Your personal system of reacting to something that happens is predicated on your mental model, not the 'goal' itself. Having an objective is important and valuable, but it won't matter if your mental model won't support it.

I mentioned the movie It's a Wonderful Life earlier in this book. The character George Bailey (Jimmy Stewart) offers us a grand illustration of how this goal vs. mental model conflict works. George Bailey had a 'goal' of leaving his hometown of Bedford Falls and getting rich. His mental model was built on values like 'thinking of others first'; which resulted in George always deferring to the aspirations of his family and friends. Moreover, he gave his money away to help others. He may have wanted to leave town and get rich, but his approach was to constantly react by helping others leave town while working for peanuts and giving away his money. He had a mental model that selflessness is all important. If he had had a mental model that thought the town and others would be fine without his help, he would have left Bedford Falls in the first five minutes of the movie.

Okay, let's get these concepts down to earth. What about you and homeschooling? Do you keep trying to reach some kind of 'goal' while thinking in ways that will never empower you to react in the ways necessary to succeed? I can almost guarantee that if you are not seeing the homeschooling results you want, it's because of the system you are using, built on your mental model(s), will never get you there. What you really need is to quit thinking about finding the right curriculum, tutor, method, or plan. Instead, you need to rebuild or renovate your mental model(s).

Building and Renovating A Mental Model:

There are four basic steps to build or renovate a mental model. Actually, almost always you are renovating; you already have some kind of model moving you to act or avoid acting to what is going on. The good news is that by reading this book, you are already on the way. Also, good courses that focus on transforming your thinking are following this approach.

In fact, that's why we recommend all of our courses at www.independenthomeschool.com; they are made to renovate your mental models! Now, while the steps are simple, they aren't always easy at first. The heavy lifting is at the beginning, but it won't last. Find your courage and give it a try. Start small if you need to, but start now. The steps are (1) Figure out your current mental model; (2) Kill it; (3) Figure out a better replacement mental model; and, (4) Make it live.

1. FIGURE OUT YOUR CURRENT MENTAL MODEL

The way to figure out your mental model is to look at your actions and ask something like, "How would I have to think life works in this area for me to act the way I do?" For example, if you allow your children to go at their own pace in math, which turns out to be a few problems a day (that they get wrong), what would you need to think? For someone to not require their students to really learn math on a regular and systematic basis, wouldn't you need to think that math doesn't matter that much? Or, maybe it does matter, but your model says some kids can do math and others can't. Another option would be that you think kids eventually have their math ability 'kick in' someday down the road. Finally, you could also think that if your kids don't like to do something, then they shouldn't have to do it (or that they'll resent you for making them do what they don't like, and so they will eventually leave you to die alone!).

You can also ask your spouse or a friend to help you figure out your mental model, how you think learning and attitude works for kids. If you keep thinking and pondering, something will make sense to you and 'feel true' — It will be a way to think that explains your actions. Your actions are the compass that will point you to the answer. If you like your actions and the results they are bringing you in your homeschool, then I wouldn't change a thing. If your actions aren't bringing you the success you want to see in an area, then find the mental model behind it. Think. Think. Think. Write it down so you can look at it and think some more. Be patient, but keep thinking. If you seek, you will find.

2. KILL IT

Once you know your basic mental model, the next step is to kill it. By 'kill it' I mean that you make it something you can no longer accept as THE TRUTH about the issue at hand. If you think some children can't learn math, then killing it would mean that you would no longer accept that conclusion as the ONLY explanation for poor math skills.

So, how do you kill it? We've discussed this skill in the section addressing your issues. Basically, you need to understand that when you have a belief that a certain mental model explains reality and predicts well, it means that you have only one way to explain what you see. Right now, wearing facemasks is a big deal, a big debate. In the middle of the coronavirus pandemic people had received all kinds of signals from the government (at first, don't wear masks, later, do wear masks). As a result, people started citing different studies to prove their point. Some insist that facemasks make a difference because it must slow down the viral load exhaled. Others insist that there is no difference, and that if they aren't the right kind and cleaned, they spread more disease or make you sick. I have friends who are intensely on one side or another. Basically, they have a mental model of face-mask-wearing. The real key is that they have only ONE story that explains reality. Face masks are an evil, false, government-deep-state ploy to train us to give up our rights. Or, masks are the key to safety and everyone who doesn't wear one is a potential murderer. I know those sound extreme, but they are actually beliefs people hold. To kill such a belief, all that is required is to learn the art of arguing with yourself. Frankly, you don't know the issue until you can argue both sides. In my experience, composing two additional stories (explanations) will kill the irrational commitment to a model. Facts can work too, but even when you find them, your mental model tends to twist or dismiss them.

Let's try it. If you think face masks are bad, then you need to think through a couple of other stories. One possible explanation is that face mask don't stop the coronavirus much, but they do bring a clearer awareness to distancing and hygiene. Another plausible story could be that they really do make a difference because a future study proves it undeniably. Another story is that it isn't about the face mask, but about helping other citizens who are naturally frightened (about ⅓ of the national bell curve) to go out of their homes and get the economy moving. If you think things like these through, and I mean really think how it is even remotely possible, you'll find that you aren't so sure about your original position. Having a little humility won't hurt you. Could you be wrong? What if you are wrong? Is there a way to be 100% sure? These questions can help kill a mental model as well. If your model withstands all this, then it might just be the right model. Of course, getting a sharp friend to help you argue against an unsupportive mental model is often a help as well. By the way, as I write this, I have no idea if masks work or not. I do know the government can require me to wear clothes, so a mask isn't a big deal to me. I also think I'm probably helping others who worry a lot. Then again, I can run out of patience; after all, I live in Texas.

If we return to our example of kids and math, then we can see the power of this approach to killing a model. Let's assume you believe that some children can't learn math; that's your model, so you try to help your child muddle through to some basic level. First off, it's odd to try to get a child to muddle through if they really can't learn the subject (sounds like torture). So, you can already see your model may not be on target. You may just think it is hard, but not impossible. Nonetheless, what are some other stories that are plausible? It could be that all children can learn math, just like all can learn to run; but only some will become Olympians. Math may be more like reading, where everyone can learn to read at some level. Yes, it is harder for some, but it isn't impossible. Another possibility is that it isn't that kids can't learn math, but that they are subjected to a method that makes it harder to do so. Just as we learned with the whole language approach to reading, bad theories can lead to bad results. It could be that learning math is like learning anything, if a child is motivated it works out. All teens can learn to drive a car, but large numbers are not learning because they are scared or don't care; Uber, right? Failure to learn a subject may not be about ability, rather it may be about motivation. Figuring out how to motivate a slow learner is a different issue than concluding they can't learn the subject at all. Finally, you may want to consider math a skill to learn. Learning a skill is hard before it's easy, but it's easy once you know how. Learning to juggle is hard at first, but is easy once you know how.

Are you better yet? You may not be, but if you think all of these possibilities through as to how they could make sense, then holding on to the ONE idea that some kids just can't learn math becomes doubtful. A doubted model won't be used much, it's dead.

3. FIGURE OUT A BETTER REPLACEMENT MENTAL MODEL

Replacing the mental model you just killed is an important step toward getting what you want. It only comes about after you have killed the old model. To discover a new mental model that will work follows the same kind of process we used earlier in discovering your current mental model. It's a little guess-work, but it's the kind of guessing that can make sense pretty quickly. (1) Begin with the result you want to see. (2) Next, consider what actions would most likely bring about that result. (3) Then, consider what these actions might be reacting to. (4) Finally, ask yourself what you'd need to be thinking, how this particular area of life would have to work, if you were going to act/react the way you need to for the result you want.

It may sound complicated, but it comes straight from the Lybrand Model itself:

Results Come from Actions; Actions Come from Choices; Choices Come from Reacting to What Your Mental Model Sees and Predicts

The steps are

1. What result do you want?

2. What actions need to happen?

3. What are these actions a reaction to?

4. What mental model would consistently see and predict these kinds of actions/reactions?

Answering these questions can help you build the model you need for the results you want. While this is the most exciting when it is done in real life, all I can offer in written form is a reasonable scenario as an example.

Let's stick with math, especially since this is a big issue for at least ½ of all homeschool students. We are assuming here that we have killed the old model that thinks some kids can't learn math at all. So, we know it is probably learnable (like reading), but we need a model to hold in mind so the right actions will lead us to success. The easiest path to take is just to walk through the questions.

1. What result do you want?

I want my student to be as competent in math as they can achieve before finishing high school. Well, that was easy enough.

2. What actions need to happen?

When we think of actions here, we need to think about you as the parent/teacher, rather than your student. If you want to think about the child's actions, then that will be a different mental model about how children learn. The actions you need are those that help the child stay engaged in learning math. The actions you need are to have the child do math daily, correct their errors, and keep doing it until they don't have errors. If you did that, wouldn't your student most likely learn math in the due course of time?

3. What are your actions a reaction to?

This one can be tricky since you can react to a lot of things in this world concerning learning math; tests, people's opinions, your moods, and math problems you don't know how to work. Most likely, the key reaction is related to your child's efforts and attitude about math. When they are upset and struggling, then you can give in and allow them not to conquer their math for the day / week / month / year. True? Your actions are a reaction to things like your own educational expectations and your child's progress or struggle.

4. What mental model would consistently see and predict these kinds of actions/reactions?

It's important to remember our working definition: **"A mental model is simply a way to think that predicts what will happen in the future, given a situation or set of circumstances."** So, we need a way to think that predicts what will happen in the future when our children react poorly or wonderfully to their efforts in learning math. How would you need to think about your role in helping a child learn math, given their different reactions? I think it comes down to a few points (this could take a little work to get to).

A. Children can, and should, teach themselves.

B. Math is a simple two-fold proposition:

    a. Math is learned incrementally. This means that there are very small steps that must be learned (once learned, they are automatic).

    b. Math is learned progressively. These increments build toward more complex things. If a child doesn't learn the basics of addition / multiplication / subtraction / division, they will simply be unable to progress to more complicated aspects of math.

    c. Therefore, a student can only learn the next thing in math; and, until that next thing is learned, there is no point in moving ahead.

C. Children need accountability to learn math daily. Most children do not find learning math enjoyable because it is a somewhat unnatural thinking process. Humans, as science has demonstrated, are especially emotional. Math on the other hand, is essentially logical. The good news is that it does feel good to us once we master it.

D. Everything is hard before it is easy, and it is easy once you know how. The teacher's role is to get them to where math is actually easy (at least for the level they achieve).

E. Success breeds success. Once a child begins to master one level, confidence builds for conquering the next level. As Emerson said, "The greater part of courage is having done it before." The aim of the teacher is to help the student notice that they are succeeding step-by-step, and to celebrate those successful efforts and results.

F. The ongoing goal is never to make my child good at math, the goal is to help make my child better at math than they were last week.

4. MAKE IT LIVE

Making it live must occur over time. Implementing your mental model is not something you do, it's something you are doing. You may not get there this week or the next, but you do get closer week by week. It basically follows the pattern of human life; conception, then development, then birth, then growth to maturity. When you make something live, you are making your actions increasingly match your thinking, your mental model. A successful maturing life is about expansion.

In our example, what would that mean if you really assumed (and even convinced yourself) that the above mental model was how learning math works? Wouldn't you start having your student work at some math each day? Would it really matter how much daily progress they made if they really learned it? If they didn't 'get it' one day, wouldn't it make sense to repeat the lesson until they did 'get it' and were confident about that one single part of math? You would probably also find a curriculum that built math incrementally, rather than dividing it by concepts. All of math is mixed together, so it's just math. A math student who is getting incrementally better is not 'good at fractions' and 'bad at factorials' are they? It is simply a matter of daily successes in learning small parts of math which build upon each other. Making it live is about you thinking consistently and acting consistently; but, getting better at it next week than you were this week. There is not a pre-made 'plan' to follow, so don't get tricked. There is simply a way to think that suggests the right actions to take. In time, you'll likely improve both your mental model and your strategic actions. That's the way it works!

If you will read this book again, take notes and review them, and dare to give up on your biggest disagreements that you can't defend, your view of educating an independent learner will be transformed.

Next, my own mental model predicts you'll see things turn out just fine.

Of course, when they grow up and think independently, they will probably do a few things you don't agree with. Then again, all kids do that; but your independent learners will have clearly thought through reasons. Honestly, that's when you've arrived. It's also when you'll touch the world for good.

The End

APPENDIX A

Tip of the Hat to Classical Education

Yes, I'd like to tip my hat to Classical Education. Frankly, had America's schools not abandoned classical education in the early part of the last century, there might be no homeschooling movement at all. If you know anything about classical education, then you'll see this book is loaded with classical education themes and practices. I love the basic idea and approach, but I also have some cautions about the classical education practices of today. Frankly, if you look at the great minds of history in Western Civilization, you'll find that these great influences were basically trained with a classical approach. It is indeed the ideology and practices (things like virtue, logic, history, and reading enduring literature) that helped produced great influential minds and characters, including almost every European and American leader (and thought leader) through WWII. We've been educating people for a long time, so the classical way is also the 'old' way. Pseudointellectuals, and I'd throw Dewey in that group, have an affinity for novelty and social engineering objectives that moved them to dismantle a system that dates back to the Aeneid, the Republic, and the Bible. Of course, studying Latin and Greek comes in handy too, if only because of the power of vocabulary. The following are a few basics to consider. The 'new' way abandons the 'old' way; hence the recovery of classical education is a strange act of rebellion that should have never been necessary.

Classical Education's Aim

The aim of classical education has always been to cultivate wise and virtuous individuals. Intellect alone has proven itself often to be either useless or dangerous. IQ elevates the elite, but wisdom does not correlate to one's intelligence quotient. Wisdom is available to any noble soul who pursues it (see Proverbs 8). Of course, an intelligent soul which is also wise benefits us all. In fact, I'd say that is an easy way to understand the importance of a classical approach to education; producing intelligent and wise individuals who can touch the world for good.

Classical education has a connection to the traditional purpose of Liberal Arts. Liberal Arts was originally about freedom. Liberal meant 'liberty' back in the day, and so the Liberal Arts were the 'freeing' arts. The point of these freeing arts was to equip the student to choose any one of a variety of paths because of a classical foundation. Harvard originally grounded students in the classics and the Bible, before they specialized in law, banking, ministry, or other. An example of this priority is seen in a couple of professors of mine who studied psychology and medicine before studying the Bible and theology. I won't go into details, but it would have been far better in reverse; thinking about psychology with a theological foundation creates a different kind of animal.

The narrow aim of classical education is to grow a student who knows how to learn. That is indeed the key. Once an individual knows how to learn, they are free to pursue the life ahead without depending on the government or thought leaders, so-called, to direct their understanding or choices. In this sense, we are desperate for classically trained thinkers in our day-and-age. Learning how to learn, along with a virtuous moral and ethical foundation, is the path to greatness...internationally, nationally, locally, or in one's most private world.

Classical Education's Process

The process itself has a little debate around it. While I appreciate the emphasis on the flow of history, Dorothy Sayers's description of the trivium works well. The stages in classical education understand that subjects involve a move from data to logic to rhetoric. Though it is described in different ways, the trivium captures the essence of learning any subject. The data is concerned with the basic information. The logic is concerned with how this information fits together. The rhetoric stage is concerned with communication and using knowledge with other human beings. Any subject one learns requires these elements and this sequence. First, you learn the vocabulary of a foreign language, then you learn the grammar (logic / how it works and fits together), and finally you use it to communicate with others. Embedded in this trivium is the parallel with human development. Until the age of 10-12, children generally love to memorize facts and poems and words. They clearly do not understand the concepts behind them (think about learning math facts without having to know why math works the way it does). Next, children start to argue and debate around ages 12-14. They are trying to 'make sense' of all the facts they've gathered so far in life. Finally, children start to become effective and persuasive in their later teens so that they can work with others in contributing to their own purpose and the great good of societal progress or sanity. All of this means that a classical approach to education is training the student to learn how to learn by moving thought the data (I know basics), to the logic (I know how it works), and to the rhetoric (I know how to communicate and use it with others). In its more detailed form, there is also the quadrivium or the 'four ways', which is comprised of arithmetic, geometry, music, and astronomy. Another approach in classical thinking might follow an emphasis on balancing science, the arts, and the gymnasium (sports).

Regardless of the exact approach, all classical learning involves reading the profound works of history while developing the skills necessary to think logically and creatively in a self-directed way. In our own approach, we applied Ockham's Lever (Chapter 2) to reduce it to the essential skill development surrounding reading, writing, and mathematics. The Robinson Curriculum served as a fine frame, to which we added our own Writing Course, Bible study, and a number of extracurricular activities, including music, art, clubs, and various sports. The Lybrand Approach is an essentials model of classical education, which puts a greater emphasis on the students' teaching themselves. It's a skill-focused, more than a merely knowledge-focused, approach to education.

Classical Education's Result

The result of the classical approach is commonly displayed with students who are simply better equipped for life. Whether it is public service, the business world, the ministry, academics, or sports competition, the student who knows how to learn is always ready for the next challenge or change. Some years ago, I ran across a study that confirmed what we all know; after only ten years, 85% of us will be in a different career path than the one we pursued in college. Today it is likely far worse, as our children will see multiple careers over time. The result of classical learning is an individual who can learn what is needed when it's needed, without having to find a trainer or a class.

Classical Education's Caution

There is a caution to consider with classical education, especially when classes, cooperatives, or schools embrace the approach. The caution is that there can be a drift away from balance into obsessive busywork. I personally believe Providence brought me to a classical understanding of education. My background in English Literature, Theology, five languages, writing, communication, law, politics, systems thinking, etc., all combined to reveal a more relaxed-and-focused way to grow independent learners. I also was a founder and instructor in a classical school (Midland Classical Academy). As I've watched life over six decades, I see a compensating drift which is often based on the notion that 'some is good, more is better'. As a result, this drift gives kids more and more work. Read more and learn more and do more is the antidote to our weakening culture. Unfortunately, this leaves the majority of kids more tired of learning than dedicated to it. I believe it is because we settle for the idea that knowledge is power. Yes, it is a kind of power, you might say it is powerful. However, KNOW HOW is where the real power is, especially when power is seen as empowerment. Knowledge is powerful, but Know How is empowering. Honing the thinking and learning skills of students allows them to access whatever knowledge they need throughout life. We printed the following and posted it in our homeschooling room:

They know enough who know how to learn. -Henry Adams

Honor simplicity, stay focused on your process, get them skill-ready, release them to the world.

A Metaphor

I mentioned that our firstborn has cerebral palsy. CP is a catchword for a category of symptoms that show up because of some kind of trauma at-or-around birth. In my son's case, he had an aneurism of some type, involving the motor strip in his brain. It showed up with spasticity on the right side of his body, making him what they call hemiplegic. Spasticity is a muscular imbalance where some muscles are getting a signal to contract all the time, while others are getting the signal to relax continuously. Since muscles need to alternate contracting and relaxing, this creates quite the challenge. Commonly, a foot will always be in the extended 'tippy toe' position. In our son's case, he eventually had to have a heel cord release so that his foot could flatten to walk with the additional help of a brace for many years.

Cerebral palsy (literally 'brain-caused-paralysis') is an inside-out problem; the brain is hurt, so the signals are skewed, the muscles are locked, and the body is eventually contorted. Much of modern education is, quite frankly, the cerebral palsy of learning. Instead of helping children who learn naturally to learn even better, the crazy stuff out there is about social agendas and self-esteem driven attempts to socially engineer the right kind of student. As a result, students are mentally crippled and paralyzed, unreasoning and busy about the business of eradicating free speech and free thought; disinterested in truth or virtue. The external solutions amount to surgery and braces to help symptoms, the real solution is to treat the heart of what makes for a great mind; learning how to learn. The head thinks profoundly and the heart lives virtuously. The hope in growing independent learners though a solid homeschool experience, is the hope of infusing clarity and light into a dark world. Classical and learn-how-to-learn methods are about light, which is eclipsed by those against classical schools, charter schools, and homeschools. We can walk straight and we can live as light in this world, if we dare grow a generation of independent learners. The strangest truth is that we already know our approach works, it has for millennia.

APPENDIX B

The 4 Magic Questions Worksheet

THE 4 MAGIC QUESTIONS WORKSHEET

1. Choose one behavioral problem
2. Start with STEP #1 and continue in order by STEPS (#1, #2, #3 ...)

3. If you don't think your answers are usable, try again after a day or two (this is a skill to learn)
4. Focus on 1 item in #4 & #5. Review impact in 1 week

1	3	4	5	2
What Do I See?	How Am I Encouraging What I see?	How Can I Discourage What I See?	How Can I Encourage What I Want To See?	What Do I Want To See?

PDF version of this chart is available at: independenthomeschool.com/4magicquestions

The Independent Homeschool

Honor simplicity, stay focused on your process, get them skill-ready, release them to the world.

For our free videos on How We Homeschool and other goodies:

www.independenthomeschool.com/freegifts

Your Personalized Notes

Your Personalized Notes

Your Personalized Notes

Your Personalized Notes

Your Personalized Notes

Made in the USA
Coppell, TX
29 December 2022

10005952R00144